ABOUT THE EDITORS

Patricia F. First is Professor of Educational Administration and Coordinator of the Program in Educational Administration, Curriculum, and Supervision at the University of Oklahoma. Professor First conducts research into legal and policy questions in educational governance. Recent articles have appeared in *Educational Evaluation and Policy Analysis*, *West's Education Law Reporter*, and the *Journal of Law and Education*.

Herbert J. Walberg is Research Professor of Education at the University of Illinois at Chicago. A member of the Educational Advisory Committee of the presidentially created New American Schools Research and Development Corporation, he served as advisor to public and private agencies in the United States and a dozen other countries on educational policy and productivity.

THE NATIONAL SOCIETY
FOR THE STUDY OF EDUCATION

The Series on Contemporary Educational Issues
Kenneth J. Rehage, Series Editor

The 1992 Titles

School Boards: Changing Local Control, Patricia F. First and
Herbert J. Walberg, editors
Restructuring the Schools: Problems and Prospects, John J. Lane and
Edgar G. Epps, editors

The Ninety-first Yearbook of the National Society for the Study of
Education, published in 1992, contains two volumes:

The Changing Contexts of Teaching, edited by Ann Lieberman
The Arts, Education, and Aesthetic Knowing, edited by Bennett Reimer
and Ralph A. Smith

All members of the Society receive its two-volume Yearbook.
Members who take the Comprehensive Membership also receive
the two current volumes in the Series on Contemporary
Educational Issues.

Membership in the Society is open to any who desire to receive its
publications. Inquiries regarding membership, including current
dues, may be addressed to the Secretary-Treasurer, NSSE, 5835
Kimbark Ave., Chicago, IL 60637.

School Boards:
Changing Local Control

Edited by

Patricia F. First
University of Oklahoma

& Herbert J. Walberg
University of Illinois at Chicago

McCutchan Publishing Corporation
P.O. Box 774, 2940 San Pablo Ave., Berkeley, CA 94702

ISBN 0–8211–0508–6
Library of Congress Catalog Card Number 91–66583

379.1531
S373f

Printed in the United States of America

251244

Contents

Section IV: How Boards See Themselves and How Their Publics See Them

Section V: From Guarding to Cheerleading: The Changing Roles of School Boards

Contributing Authors

Joseph M. Cronin, President, Bentley College

Jaqueline P. Danzberger, Director, Governance Programs, The Institute for Educational Leadership

C. Emily Feistritzer, President, National Center for Education Information

Chester E. Finn, Jr., Professor, Education and Public Policy, Vanderbilt University and Director, Educational Excellence Network

Patricia F. First, Professor, Department of Educational Leadership and Policy Studies, University of Oklahoma

Louis F. Miron, Director, Urban Educational Laboratory and Assistant Professor, Department of Educational Leadership and Foundations, University of New Orleans

Sally Bulkley Pancrazio, Professor and Chair, Department of Educational Administration and Foundations, Illinois State University

Charles J. Russo, Assistant Professor, Division of Administration, Policy and Urban Education, Fordham University

Thomas A. Shannon, Executive Director, National School Boards Association

Michael D. Usdan, President, The Institute for Educational Leadership and Adjunct Professor, Fordham University

Herbert J. Walberg, Research Professor of Education, University of Illinois at Chicago

Robert K. Wimpelberg, Associate Dean, College of Education, and Associate Professor, Department of Educational Leadership and Foundations, University of New Orleans

Preface

It is an age of educational restructuring. As the 1990s opened, President George Bush and the fifty governors set forth national goals for education; and the National Assessment Governing Board formulated national achievement levels to be assessed. In 1991, America 2000 set forth a bold plan to establish a million-dollar model school in each of the 535 congressional districts. Also created was the New American Schools Research and Development Corporation, which aimed to raise $200 million to restructure schools and school districts. In the meantime, state legislators and state school boards have mandated radical reforms, partly because they are providing a greater share of school funding, and school funds constitute an ever larger share of state budgets. At the same time, school-site management, teacher "empowerment," and local school councils (as in Chicago) have devolved financial and governing authority to the school level. In the midst of these extraordinary national, state, and school initiatives, what is the role of America's traditional institution—the local school board?

At the local level, a board of lay citizens, commonly called the local school board, has been traditionally expected to be the policymaking entity for the schools. Given pressures from the federal and state levels of educational governance, what is left for local boards? It is a fair question, and is in fact one of the most important structural issues in educational governance in the first years of the 1990s.

More than fifteen thousand school boards meet regularly to determine policy for American education. (As a result of consolidation of school districts, the number of school boards has decreased markedly since 1947 when there were close to ninety-five thousand districts nationwide.) As told by the National School Board Association, the school board story is impressive. School board members have educational responsibility for nearly 40 million students, fiscal responsibilities for more than $160 billion each year, and responsibility as the employer of nearly 4 million individuals. Almost 4 percent of the U.S. gross national product goes to expenditures for elementary and secondary education.

In just one state, Illinois, close to a thousand school boards, composed of some seven thousand elected citizens, gather in three-hour-plus school board meetings twelve to twenty-six times annually. And these districts vary widely in size and type and in the quality of education they offer.

Wide-ranging differences of opinion regarding the efficacy and importance of local school boards are explored in this book. Belief in local control and keeping power "close to the people," at the "grass roots" level, is a deeply held American value. We are distinctive in the developed world in allowing over fifteen thousand groups of private citizens to make hiring, firing, and curricular decisions about the education of the country's youth. That a child's education can differ from community to community confounds visitors from other countries.

The powers of school boards seem broad to the public. And in fact, when there are challenges to decisions made by school boards, courts do tend to uphold the school boards, and have done so in an overwhelming number of recent legal challenges to new educational practices.

Nevertheless, local school boards are creatures of legislatures, created as instrumentalities to carry out a decidedly state function, the provision of public education. Whether they are appointed or elected, school board members are state, not local, officers. Even where school board members are appointed by a mayor, they are still state, not municipal, officers, although certain aspects of governance may be delegated to local authorities. Local school board members hold office by virtue of legislative enactment, and their powers may be extended or limited at the discretion of the state legislature.

School boards also cultivate relations with other layers of government. In any geographic location, school governments and general
local governments may overlap. Relations are easily strained, and
disputes are frequently brought before the courts. School boards can
do what the legislatures in their states have authorized them to do.
These are called the expressed powers of the board. But legislatures
cannot foresee every eventuality, and therefore school boards also
have implied powers, that is, the powers necessary to accomplish the
tasks of the expressed powers. In this large gray area of implied
powers, there is room for disagreement, and thus much litigation and
public debate.

Boards cannot delegate away their powers, but they can establish
policies and procedures to be carried out by superintendents. The
degree and areas of delegation vary under different state laws and are
another area of frequent dispute.

In exercising their powers, school boards must respond to a wide
range of interested parties with a wide range of viewpoints. The core
groups include parents, students, teachers, taxpayers, minorities, and
the federal and state governments. These groups pressure school
boards on a variety of issues, some of which conflict. They make
demands on school boards as the boards wield both their expressed
and implied powers.

In the context of such national, state, and local pressure, this book
explores the changing roles and forms of American school boards. The
following overview of this volume will highlight some of these pressures and policy responses.

OVERVIEW

The book is divided into five sections. In the first section, Charles
Russo's chapter, "The Legal Status of School Boards in the Intergovernmental System," starts with the point that local boards are
agents of state boards but do not have complete discretion in governance and operations—a source of tension in an age of reform. He
reviews the early history of boards, and documents legal precedents
for determining authority of state and local boards and state courts.
He concludes with a perspective on the governance of local boards in
the light of current efforts to devolve considerable operational authority to the school level.

The second section of the book contains a debate about the need for school boards. In Chapter 2, "Reinventing Local Control," Chester E. Finn, Jr., provocatively challenges conventional wisdom about the value of local boards. He likens them to middle management that may be not only redundant with state and school authorities but an expensive obstacle to effective communication between them. Since much of the educational reform and restructuring effort is taking place at the state level, school boards have little to add and may be a drag on accountability and change. Although an American tradition, they are not part of the U.S. Constitution and might, he argues, best be abolished.

In his reply, "Local Control and 'Organizacrats,'" Thomas A. Shannon finds Finn's reasons for abolishing boards off the mark. Even though states are picking up a greater share of school costs, he sees no reason that local board autonomy should be diminished. Nor does he see local school boards lagging in innovation; they are, he argues, merely more difficult for the press to cover. He cites what he believes are indispensable functions of local boards.

The third section of the volume focuses on urban problems and state pressures on school boards. In "Reallocating the Power of Urban School Boards," Joseph Cronin reviews the restructuring of boards and systems in Chelsea (Massachusetts), Chicago, and New York. He begins with the rich history of organizational failure in New York City. As he points out, the scandal and inefficiency of the past provide impetus for continuing effort to reorganize under the present superintendent, Joseph Fernandez. Chicago provides perhaps the most striking and comprehensive current plan. Cronin chronicles the historical reasons for Chicago's radicalism and describes the recent status of its reform. He also discusses the Chelsea plan, in which Boston University is, in effect, provisionally assuming responsibility for operational duties of the board. In his concluding section, Cronin draws implications of his findings for further planning.

In her chapter, "State Takeovers and Other Last Resorts," Sally Pancrazio defines and describes "takeovers" of malfunctioning local districts. Although the term formerly applied to financial matters, it now applies in addition to districts that are failing to meet academic standards. A chief state school officer may remove local board members, appoint a community advisory board, and replace the chief local administrators. Pancrazio discusses the four arguments for state takeovers, including the need for children's interests to remain paramount in school decisions.

The fourth section deals with how school boards see themselves and how their publics see them. The chapter by Jacqueline P. Danzberger and Michael Usdan, "Strengthening a Grass Roots American Institution: The School Board," summarizes the findings and implications of an extensive study of state and local school boards. They first review the contemporary political environment before turning to the results of their study, which suggest fifteen indicators of school board effectiveness. School boards, they find, clearly need to improve their leadership and operational effectiveness. Among the areas of needed improvement are creating linkages with general government and children's services, improving accountability, setting of priorities, and getting parental and community involvement.

In "A Profile of School Board Presidents," C. Emily Feistritzer shows that these community leaders are usually white, male, and in their late forties. They have more education, earn more, and are more conservative than the average American. Most are satisfied with their decision-making powers, but two-thirds agree that involving parents more directly would improve the educational system. Yet while the public strongly favors the idea of letting parents choose their children's school, only 36 percent of the presidents and 31 percent of the superintendents agree.

The final section of the volume deals with the changing roles of school boards. In their chapter, "The Role of School Boards in the Governance of Education," Louis Miron and Robert Wimpelberg assert that the degree of local board control depends on the allocation of state funds for local educational spending. For this reason, they review recent litigation on state and local financing of education. To explain current policy dilemmas, they cite the political science bargaining models of Paul Peterson: pluralistic bargaining involves electoral and organizational interest; ideological bargaining hinges on broader policy issues such as school choice. Given the requirements of schools, local boards must play various political roles such as legitimator and patronizer. In the present age of reform, however, the authors argue that school boards have the opportunity to put politics aside and to increase the effectiveness and efficiency of the schools in their jurisdictions.

In the final chapter, "Evaluating School Boards: Looking Through Next-Generation Lenses," Patricia First begins with an examination of how boards have been traditionally evaluated. She then turns to new empirical studies of boards' functioning and demographic composition, especially as contrasted to those they serve. In particular, she discusses new plans in which boards set broad goals to be attained by schools and then evaluate their attainment—on the model of business decentralization. Her own research shows the large changes in the substance of school board meetings during a recent period of educational reform. In conclusion, she asks how boards may best serve students in the next decade.

Given the educational reforms in the 1980s and the restructuring of the early 1990s, we hope that policymakers, educators, and the general public will be interested in the changing forms and functions of local school boards. And we hope that with the information and commentary presented in this book, they will be in a better position to understand the context of substantive changes that will take place in the education system through the remainder of the decade.

Patricia F. First
Herbert J. Walberg

Section I

Legal Issues

CHAPTER 1

The Legal Status of School Boards in the Intergovernmental System

Charles J. Russo

INTRODUCTION

Perhaps the most unique aspect of American public education is local control by lay school boards. Yet, because the tradition of local control is so deeply rooted in American history, with its origins in first-generation colonial Massachusetts, the legal theory addressing the function and authority of school boards is not always well understood. In other words, there is a paradox present in the fact that while local school boards as the governing bodies of school districts are agents of the state responsible for local education, they are not free to exercise unfettered discretion on behalf of their local constituencies; they must act within the parameters established by the state. In light of this tension and the recent focus on school reform at the local level, I provide in this chapter a legal analysis of the role of school boards in the American intergovernmental system.

After an overview of the history and development of local school boards, I examine their sources of authority. I then consider boards as creatures of the state both as quasi-corporate municipal entities and as agents of the state. In the next section, I review the legal duties of school boards. I then turn to an examination of the evolving status of school boards in light of school-based management. Boards are increasingly engaging in participative decision making with their teachers, and in the final section of this chapter, I consider two successful programs involving shared decision making and raise questions about the limitations that states may impose on the power of school boards to delegate their decision-making authority to school-based advisory councils.

HISTORICAL OVERVIEW OF THE DEVELOPMENT OF SCHOOL BOARDS

From the earliest days of colonial New England, education was among the first concerns of the colonists. In 1642, a Massachusetts law called on "certain chosen men of each town to ascertain from time to time, if parents and masters were attending to their educational duties; if the children were being trained in learning and labor and other employments." After five years, however, the law was abandoned as unsatisfactory (Johns, Morphet, and Alexander, 1983, p. 2), for it did not mandate the establishment of public schools.

A second law, passed in 1647, was more successful. The "ye old deluder" law, so called because it was designed to combat Satan and his desire to delude people into ignorance of scriptures in order to more easily lead them to damnation, required all towns to establish and maintain public schools. Towns not observing the law were to be fined. While this law was not strictly complied with only a decade after its enactment, due in large part to the growth of private schools, it is an important law because it introduced the principle that education is a function of local government. Moreover, virtually the same law was introduced in Connecticut in 1650 (Cremin, 1970, pp. 181–182). In 1693, local control over education was further solidified through the enactment of a law that called on towns and their selectmen to jointly maintain the schools; it also mandated the imposition of taxes to support the schools if so directed by a vote of the residents at a town meeting (Reeves, 1954, p. 19). Similar laws were soon in effect throughout the New England colonies.

Early American public education thus was a function of local government, first administered through town meetings and later, as towns grew larger, under the control of town selectmen. However, since the selectmen were responsible for all town agencies, not only education, they often delegated authority for such tasks as choosing a new teacher or supervising the construction of a new school building. When it became necessary for selectmen to delegate more and more of their duties relating to educational matters, the first permanent School Committee was appointed in 1721 in Boston; this marks the beginning of the process of separating school governing bodies from other local governmental entities (Reeves, 1954, p. 17).

The colonial practice of local control was carried over into the new American republic. In 1789, a Massachusetts law authorized the creation of separate "School Committees." Later that year, a Boston law called for the election of a twelve-member committee to serve as a separate governing body over public education (Callahan, 1975, p. 19). In 1798, Massachusetts recognized the committees as separate governing bodies, but selectmen or other town officials were sometimes members of the board. Consequently, in 1826, the law was amended to ensure that these committees were independent of other governmental bodies (Reeves, 1954, p. 20). In this way, the process begun over a century earlier was brought to completion. Contemporaneously, two significant developments took place on the national scene.

Article III of the Northwest Ordinance, adopted in 1787, provided that "religion, morality, and knowledge, being necessary to good government and the happiness of mankind, schools and the means of education shall forever be encouraged" (Rotunda, Nowak, and Young, 1986, p. 544). This language greatly influenced several state constitutions in the Midwest and is evident today where states grant plenary powers to local school boards.

In 1791, the Bill of Rights was ratified. The Tenth Amendment to the Constitution states: "The powers not delegated to the United States by the Constitution, nor prohibited by it to the States, are reserved to the States respectively, or to the people." Since education is not specifically delegated to the federal government, it is under state control. The Tenth Amendment, however, does not preclude all federal involvement in education. In fact, one need only look at such far-ranging federal legislation as Titles VI and VII of the Civil Rights Act of 1964, or at PL 94–142 (the Education for All Handicapped Children Act) to recognize the substantial federal presence in education. These federal incursions notwithstanding, each state, acting through its legislature, has delegated administrative authority to local school boards to operate the schools through professional personnel hired to supervise and direct the educational enterprise.

Two subsequent developments are worthy of brief mention: the superintendency and the judicial interpretation of evolving school board authority. Until 1837 and the creation of the first superintendencies in Buffalo and Louisville (Reller, 1935, pp. 81–82), school boards performed executive, administrative, and legislative tasks that they were largely unqualified to handle. By delegating some of their authority to a superintendent of schools, the boards were able to devote their time and energy to larger policy issues by relieving themselves of such day-to-day concerns as the supervision of instruction (the primary focus of most early superintendents) and the evaluation of schools. Thus, the boards retained the legal authority to operate the schools while entrusting more mundane duties of school management to trained employees answerable to the school boards.

In *Stuart v. School District Number 1 of the Village of Kalamazoo* (1874), the Supreme Court of Michigan upheld the decision of the local school board to maintain a high school even though it lacked express legislative authority to do so. Although this case is most often cited for its importance with regard to the establishment of free, tax-supported secondary schools, it is also of great significance for school boards. It stands for the proposition that local boards have implied power to act as they deem appropriate in matters of educational policy and school governance. With this ruling as a backdrop, then, I now turn to an examination of the sources of school board authority.

SOURCES OF SCHOOL BOARD AUTHORITY

The local school board acts as an agent of the state in the complex web of intergovernmental relations, and there are two distinct dimensions to its exercise of authority: formal and informal. While the formal dimension provides a school board with the legal authority to act, the informal relates to a board's ability to influence through its capacity to shape decisions by informal means. An effective school board needs both legal authority and influence, the sources of which I will consider in this section.

Operating within the system of checks and balances designed to ensure that no one of the three coequal branches of government exercises more authority than the others, a school board's legal authority is derived from and influenced by four related legal sources: constitutional provisions, state legislative enactments, state rules and regulations, and judicial and administrative interpretations. Before examining these sources, I have one caveat: Each of the fifty states has established its own network of structures to regulate education. Consequently, the information presented here is of a general nature and may not exactly describe the education regulatory structure in all states.

The constitutions of all fifty states contain broadly worded provisions that vest authority over public education in their legislatures. Except for general constitutional principles that protect individual rights and liberties or impose a nondelegable ministerial duty on the legislature, such as to establish a public school system, state constitutions vest total control over education in their legislatures, with generally no limits.

A local school board and the district in its charge are creatures of the state; they may be created or abolished by the will of the legislature. Concomitantly, state legislatures exercise plenary power over education through statutory enactments or laws; they may enact any legislation that is neither expressly nor implicitly forbidden by the state constitution (Edwards, 1955, p. 27). This generally accepted principle is reflected in an opinion by the Michigan Supreme Court: "The legislature has entire control over the schools of the state. . . . The division of the territory of the state into districts, the conduct of the schools, the qualifications of the teachers, the subjects to be taught therein, are all within its control" (*Child Welfare Society of Flint v. Kennedy School District*, 1922, p. 296).

Although laws regulating public education through local school boards vary from state to state, all states dictate such matters as the corporate nature and size of local boards as well as the powers delegated to them. In this way, board responsiveness to legislative control is ensured; at the same time, the legislature places a limit on the power boards may exercise apart from that explicitly vested in them by statute. (In a later section of this chapter, I detail the specifics of board responsibilities.) The legislature, then, has the authority to devise broad statements of educational policy while delegating the responsibility for implementing its will to state and local educational agencies.

Since it is virtually impossible for state legislatures to exercise their control over education on a daily basis, they have conferred administrative rule-making and some limited policymaking authority on subordinate agencies and officials; they are forbidden by constitutional provisions to delegate their legislative authority. State boards of education, acting in concert with either a commissioner of education or state superintendent for public instruction, are present in forty-nine states and are responsible for the general supervision of public education in the state; only Wisconsin does not have such a board. As an adjunct to state boards, thirty-four states also maintain departments of education. These departments share in carrying out those tasks that the state boards, in conjunction with their legislatures and chief executive officers, determine to be in the best educational interests of the people of the state. State education departments are typically responsible for such matters as planning and implementing instructional programs, establishing high school graduation requirements, establishing certification standards for teachers and administrators, and compiling and analyzing educational statistics (Wiles and Bondi, 1985). The powers delegated to the state board are generally coextensive with those exercised by local school boards and help to ensure the efficient administration of public education.

When a dispute arises over the interpretation or application of a law or administrative regulation, differences of opinion can be resolved either through administrative channels or in the courts. Administrative challenges are ordinarily brought to the state attorney general's office, which has the authority to interpret these rules for school districts and other state agencies; some states, such as New York, assign this duty to the state commissioner's office. Unless such a review establishes that a decision was "arbitrary and capricious," it will be upheld. Moreover, administrative review is subject to the exhaustion-of-remedies doctrine, under which an individual who presents a challenge in the courts without first exhausting all administrative appeals forfeits all subsequent administrative appeals. This procedure is intended to ensure that adequate review is provided by the appropriate state agencies and to avoid seeking recourse with the courts over issues that are primarily administrative, not legal.

The courts do not ordinarily interfere with the actions of a school board (or other educational agencies) unless there is a clear abuse of discretion or a violation of the law. In reviewing the actions of a board, courts apply the substantial-evidence rule. This common-law rule limits a court's review of an administrative decision to a determination of whether the decision was based on substantial evidence; if a court finds that it was, then it will ordinarily look no further. An opinion by an appellate court in Illinois cogently reflects these widely accepted legal principles:

> A court of review cannot substitute its judgment for the judgment of the administrative tribunal. The question is not simply whether the court of review agrees or disagrees with the finding below. It has been said that courts should not disturb administrative findings unless such findings are arbitrary, or constitute an abuse of discretion, or are without substantial foundation in evidence, or are obviously and clearly wrong, or unless an opposite conclusion is clearly evident. [*Board of Education v. County Board of School Trustees* (1961), p. 635]

In a challenge to a board's actions, the burden of proof, of course, rests on the individual bringing the charge. Further, given the reluctance of the courts to reverse administrative decisions, at least one state court has ruled that any allegations of abuse of discretion must be established by "clear and convincing evidence" (*Safferstone v. Tucker*, 1962, p. 4), which is a higher standard than the preponderance of the evidence ordinarily called for in civil actions. Thus, provided that a school board properly exercises those narrowly defined powers expressly delegated to it by law, or acts in a manner that is reasonably implied by or is incidental to this authority, or acts in a fashion that is essential to the accomplishment of the objectives of the school, then the courts are not likely to intervene.

Local boards' legal authority to operate the schools is only one dimension of their power. Given their crucial place in the complex array of social and intergovernmental structures, school boards and their members must be sensitive to the needs of their communities and must learn to temper legal authority through the exercise of influence, which "deals with the capacity to shape decisions through informal or nonauthoritative means" (Conley, 1989, p. 368). Clearly, school boards have a legal right and duty to run the schools, but when a school board (and school district) is confronted by an issue that divides the community, the unilateral exercise of its legal authority may not be in the best interest of the community. Under such circumstances, a board should exercise its symbolic leadership through the assertion of influence, whether by individual board members or as a group. By exercising influence rather than legal authority, a board can seek to form a consensus and can thereby unite the community behind a particular course of action. Hence, the more proficient a school board is at exercising the different dimensions of its authority, the broader its base of support will be and the more effective it should become.

As important as the influence of the board or an individual board member may be, school boards are creatures of the state and, as such, must act accordingly. Thus, I consider next the school board as a creature of the state.

THE SCHOOL BOARD: A CREATURE OF THE STATE

A local school board is typically a quasi-municipal corporation, or political subdivision of the state, created for the sole purpose of administering a public school district. An agent of the state, a local board is responsible for carrying out the mandate entrusted to it by the state legislature; it has no inherent authority apart from that vested in it by the legislature. While it addressed a municipal corporation rather than a more limited quasi-municipal corporation, the words of the Supreme Court of Washington succinctly describe the power of a local board:

> It is a general and undisputed proposition of law that a municipal corporation possesses and can exercise the following powers and no others: First, those granted in express words; second, those necessarily or fairly implied in or incident to the powers expressly granted; third, those essential to the declared objectives and purposes of the corporation—not simply convenient but indispensable. Any fair or reasonable doubt concerning the existence of power is resolved by the courts against the corporation and the power is denied. [McGilvra v. School District (1921), p. 818]

A member of the body politic, a school board is a continuous corporate entity that exists apart from the individuals sitting on it at any one time. And because a school board has perpetual succession, a change in its membership does not alter its legal status. Consequently, the legality of its contracts is not conditioned by the official life of its members (Hamilton and Reutter, 1958, pp. 5–6). In addition to being able to enter into contracts, school boards enjoy a wide variety of legal rights, including the rights to hire and fire personnel, to sue and to be sued, and to own property.

Members of a school board are state, not local, officials (*State ex rel. Walsh v. Hine*, 1890; *Landis v. School District Number 44*, 1895). Even where the boundaries of a school district and a municipality are the same, their affairs are separate (*State ex rel. Harbach v. Mayor of the City of Milwaukee*, 1925). Yet, a board is regarded as a local political entity by the residents of its district and must be responsive to their needs. Since better than 90 percent of school boards are elected, board members need not wonder about whether they are responsive to local needs, for they will find out at the polls (Danzberger et al., 1987, p. 54).

In order for a school board to act, it must do so in its corporate capacity; its proposed actions must be expressed by a resolution or a motion accepted by a majority of its members. The importance of a board's exercise of corporate authority is highlighted by the fact that courts have consistently ruled that board transactions not entered into at a formal board meeting have no legal effect (New York State School Boards Association, 1988, p. 9–2.10; *Aikman v. School District Number 16*, 1882).

Individual members are not permitted to exercise the corporate authority of the board. Board members who act in their own name may be held personally liable for any acts that exceed the board's authority or that are not performed in good faith; members may also be held individually liable for good-faith actions of the board that exceed its authority or if it acts illegally (Nolte, 1984).

A school board can neither divest itself of the powers entrusted to it by statute nor delegate its discretionary power to subcommittees, its employees, or other governmental agencies. This does not prevent a board from establishing subcommittees to conduct preliminary work or fact-finding as long as final determinations are rendered by the board as a whole (Reutter, 1985).

Although a school board is a quasi-municipal corporation, a typical board is organized like a private corporation. This "top down" structural arrangement is a direct result of the educational reform movement of the late nineteenth century toward centralization, which sought to guarantee standards and quality for all students (Tyack, 1974; Cooper, 1989). By way of analogy, the residents of a district (and state) are the shareholders or owners of the corporation; the school board is the board of directors that acts on behalf of the shareholders; the superintendent is the chief executive officer; central office administrators are officers; and the teachers and staff are the employees.

While a corporate style of decision making appears to have served

most school boards and districts well in the past and is supported by
the great weight of legal precedent, the principle of corporate consolidation with authority vested in one executive officer oftentimes fails to
recognize that the superintendent is an employee of the board. This
oversight frequently reduces school boards to forgotten players in
educational reform. At the same time, it may be argued that a school
board that has lost its authority is more at fault than the superintendent. In other words, a board may, due to its unwillingness to lead
or its desire to pursue an agenda different from that of the superintendent, find its authority seriously compromised. Either way, though, it
has virtually been reduced to spectator status in the educational
arena. However, as board-superintendent relations present an ongoing dilemma that may be more a question of group dynamics and
local politics (Cistone, 1975) than a question of law, I investigate here
a more timely concern for school boards. More specifically, consistent
with the current wave of school reform, it may be time for a new
organizational paradigm to emerge, one that acknowledges the vital
contribution boards have to offer by working more collegially with the
professional educators in their employ. For such a metamorphosis to
occur, legal changes will have to take place. The changes necessary to
implement such an innovation are explored in the final section of this
chapter, where I examine the future of boards in light of school-based
management.

THE DUTIES OF A LOCAL SCHOOL BOARD

There are three dimensions to a local school board's exercise of its
legal authority: executive, legislative, and quasi-judicial. A board uses
executive power when it enters into contracts with personnel or for
services. It employs legislative authority when it determines district
policy and approves rules and regulations necessary to carry out its
policy. Examples of legislative authority include student dress codes
and "no pass, no play" rules for student athletes. A board functions in
a quasi-judicial manner when it hears appeals resulting from the
implementing of its policies.

The three dimensions of a school board's powers are carried out
through the exercise of two distinct types of legal actions, discretionary and ministerial duties. At times it may be difficult to distinguish

between these two categories of acts, but they are sufficiently different to allow for a delineation of the legal principles involved.

Discretionary power "gives the board the power to act in the event that it chooses to do so" (Goldhammer, 1964, p. 58). Discretionary functions involve desirable rather than mandatory activities and arguably account for the larger part of a board's actions (Campbell et al., 1990, p. 208). Examples of discretionary power include the right to expand the size of a school's professional staff, to decide whether to accept federal aid for school programs, and to require curricular modifications and standards that may be more stringent than state guidelines. And as discussed earlier, provided that a board properly exercises its discretionary power (that is, its actions are neither arbitrary nor capricious), the courts are reluctant to interfere with its actions.

Ministerial or mandatory functions are those "which the law imposes upon the board and which it must perform regardless of the presence of any condition which, in the minds of the members of the board, would indicate a desirability not to act" (Goldhammer, 1964, p. 59). Failure of a board to exercise its ministerial responsibilities may result in corporate and/or personal liability by the board and its members. State laws relating to mandatory board authority range from general to specific. Typical mandatory board duties include obligations to adopt bylaws and rules to discharge board duties, to hire a superintendent and other school personnel, to purchase sites on which to build schools, to prescribe courses of instruction and textbooks, and to enforce compulsory state education laws (*McKinney's Consolidated Laws of New York, Education Law*, Sec. 1709, 1990). A ministerial function allows for little or no choice concerning whether or how it is to be performed.

The line between mandatory and discretionary duties can be a fine one and is easily blurred. For example, while state law mandates the length of the school year, a local board has discretion to rely on its administrative staff to establish its district's calendar and to determine the days on which the schools are to be in session.

A board, however, cannot delegate its authority to act in matters that the legislature specifically assigns it. For example, a board alone has the authority to hire teachers. Since it is impractical, if not impossible, for a board to be actively involved in the process of hiring all new teachers, it must rely on its administrative staff to make recommendations concerning the suitability of prospective teachers.

Then, even if a board's approval is merely a formality, it will have carried out its legal mandate. In light of the emergence of school-based management and new working relationships between school boards and building-level management councils concerning personnel, budgetary, and curricular matters, it will be interesting to observe the changes in the relationships between school boards and their professional staffs.

THE FUTURE OF SCHOOL BOARDS IN LIGHT OF SCHOOL-BASED MANAGEMENT

The current wave of school reform urges the restructuring of public education by making the schools more flexible and amenable to change (Timar, 1990). Concomitantly, there is also a call to move away from centralized bureaucracies to site-based management (Cooper, 1990). Among those highlighting the need for such change is the Carnegie Task Force on Teaching as a Profession: "School systems based on bureaucratic authority must be replaced by schools in which authority is grounded in the professional roles of teachers" (1986, p. 55). It continues on to say that "districts should foster collegial styles of decision making and teaching in schools" (p. 56). If this call to reform is to be adopted, the trick is to provide building-level professionals with a greater role in the daily operations of the schools while preserving the legal integrity and authority of local school boards.

While the ultimate responsibility for operating public schools remains with local school boards, they may delegate some of their authority to the teaching and administrative staff, provided they do so in accordance with the wishes of their state legislatures. Two fine examples of shared decision making between school boards and their teachers are the Rochester (New York) and Toledo (Ohio) school systems (Rauth, 1990), which delegated some authority to teachers and their unions to help evaluate and work with fellow teachers who were not performing adequately, a traditional responsibility of the administrative staff. But even their programs have not been implemented without difficulty.

The Peer Assistance and Review plan (PAR), enacted pursuant to New York state education law, was entered into by agreement between the teachers' union and the Rochester City School District.

PAR, which calls for the assessment and evaluation of intern teachers by members of the full-time teaching staff, was challenged by a principal in Rochester. She claimed that PAR had a harmful effect on her administrative duties and responsibilities by its contravention of the nondiscretionary mandate of state law. A New York appellate court rejected her challenge, reasoning that PAR neither limited the duty of school administrators to evaluate classroom teachers nor had the harmful effect that she alleged (*Carnahan v. McWalters*, 1988). Since the question of the board's authority to include such a provision in the teachers' contract had not been raised, the court did not address it.

A similar peer evaluation plan sponsored by the Toledo Federation of Teachers and the Toledo Public Schools also muddled the line between managerial and nonmanagerial responsibilities (Walters and Wyatt, 1985). The program exposed school districts to complaints of unfair labor practices by teachers dismissed as a result of unfavorable peer evaluations. A statute seeking to insulate schools from liability while permitting the expansion of similar programs faced opposition from an unlikely source, the Ohio Education Association, a powerful and much larger teachers' union, despite the fact that its largest local has adopted a similar program. The passage of this bill by the Ohio legislature (Schmidt, 1990) coupled with the ruling in New York bodes well for the future of similar shared decision-making plans.

Given the fact that teachers are becoming increasingly interested in and involved in managing their schools (David, 1989), school boards, teachers, and administrators have a wonderful opportunity to work together to improve public education. Yet, the opportunity presented by school-based management cannot be embraced without caution, for it raises significant legal and policy questions. For example, how much of a school board's authority can be shared with site-based management councils? By what means can a board's authority be shared with these councils? Are states willing to reverse the long-held American tradition of lay control over local education by vesting full authority for the educational enterprise in the professional staff?

As much as there may be a need to consider new organization paradigms for school leadership in some localities, especially in large urban centers where school boards are, at best, accountable to no one and, at worst, ineffectual, such a major change cannot be undertaken without first considering the ramifications. To do otherwise would wreak havoc in the schools. For example, if school boards, even with the approval of their legislatures, delegate increasing responsibility to school staffs, who will retain legal accountability for the schools? How much control will localities retain over education? What role might the state assume in overseeing the schools?

If, as supporters of school-based management suggest, the principal, rather than the school board, becomes the central focus of any transfer of authority, then the board's role is not likely to be altered significantly, as the nexus of change will take place in the relationship between the school site and central office. In fact, as long as the board retains its primary responsibility of providing broad policy goals and directions for the district and avoids becoming actively involved in the daily activities of the schools, then a shift to school-based management should leave the board essentially unaffected. If anything, a shift to school-based management may even expand the board's authority, as Paul Cunningham, a board member in Cambridge, Maryland, has noted: "When the board makes the decision to decentralize the decision-making process, it is exercising policy development of the highest order" (Lindelow and Heynderickx, 1989, p. 124). Oron South, a consultant to the Monroe County (Florida) Schools went even further when he pointed out that rather than limit a board's sense of control over the schools, school-based management expands it by providing board members with "a greater sense of power—not so much to order people around, but finally to get something done" (Lindelow and Heynderickx, 1989, p. 125). Thus, far from limiting the board's authority, a shift to local control may further enhance it.

If the initial stages in the growth of school-based management throughout the county serve as a guide, it appears that any wholesale changes in board operations are not likely to be accomplished by judicial fiat. Rather, major innovations will occur through legislative action. And, given the typically slow speed of the legislative process, it may be some time before any large-scale changes actually take place. And many politicians and educators may be reluctant to recognize and accept the need to change.

Regardless of the outcome of these questions, the 1990s should be an exciting time for all those involved with education, as a new balance of power may be emerging in board-staff relations. For school boards themselves, the answers to these questions take on an even greater significance, because their very futures may depend on them.

REFERENCES

Aikman v. School District Number 16, 27 Kan. 129 (1882).

Board of Education of Libertyville-Fremont Consolidated High School Number 120 of Lake County v. County Board of School Trustees of Lake County, 176 N.E.2d 633 (Ill. 1961).

Callahan, Raymond E. "The American Board of Education, 1789–1960." In *Understanding School Boards*, edited by Peter J. Cistone. Lexington, Mass.: Lexington Books, 1975.

Campbell, Roald F.; Cunningham, Luvern L.; Nystrand, Raphael O.; and Usdan, Michael D. *The Organization and Control of American Schools*, 3d ed. Columbus, Ohio: Merrill Publishing Co., 1990.

Carnahan v. McWalters, 536 N.Y.S.2d 345 (App. Div. 1988).

Carnegie Task Force on Teaching as a Profession. *A Nation Prepared: Teachers for the 21st Century*. New York: Carnegie Forum on Education and the Economy, 1986.

Child Welfare Society of Flint v. Kennedy School District, 189 N.W. 1002 (Mich. 1922).

Cistone, Peter J., ed. *Understanding School Boards*. Lexington, Mass.: Lexington Books, 1975.

Conley, Sharon C. "'Who's on First?' School Reform, Teacher Participation, and the Decision-making Process," *Education and Urban Society* 21, no. 4 (1989): 366–379.

Cooper, Bruce S. "Bottom-up Authority in School Organization: Implications for the School Administrator," *Education and Urban Society* 21, no. 4 (1989): 380–392.

Cooper, Bruce S. "Unions, Central Management, and School-site Control: Is a New Organizational Paradigm in the Making?" Paper presented at the annual convention of the University Council on Educational Administration, Pittsburgh, Penn., 1990.

Cremin, Lawrence A. *American Education: The Colonial Experience*, 1607–1783. New York: Harper and Row, 1970.

Danzberger, Jacqueline P.; Carol, Lila N.; Cunningham, Luvern L.; Kirst, Michael W.; McCloud, Barbara A.; and Usdan, Michael D. "School Boards: The Forgotten Players on the Education Team," *Phi Delta Kappan* 69, no. 1 (1987): 53–59.

David, Jane L. "Synthesis of Research on School-based Management," *Educational Leadership* 46, no. 8 (1989): 45–53.

Edwards, Newton. *The Courts and the Public Schools*. Chicago: University of Chicago Press, 1955.

Goldhammer, Keith. *The School Board*. New York: Center for Applied Research in Education, 1964.

Hamilton, Robert R., and Reutter, E. Edmund. *Legal Aspects of School Board Operations*. New York: Teachers College, Columbia University, 1958.

Johns, Roe L.; Morphet, Edgar L., and Alexander, Kern. *The Economics of School Finance*, 4th ed. Englewood Cliffs, N.J.: Prentice-Hall, 1983.

Landis v. School District Number 44, 31 A. 1017 (N. J. 1895).

Lindelow, J. and Heynderickx, J. "School-based Management." In *School Leadership: Handbook for Excellence*, 2d ed., edited by S. C. Smith and P. K. Piele. Eugene: ERIC Clearinghouse, University of Oregon, 1989.

McGilvra v. School District, 194 P. 817 (Wash. 1921).

McKinney's Consolidated Laws of New York, Annotated, Education Law, Sec. 1709. St. Paul, Minn.: West Publishing Co., 1990.

New York State School Boards Association. *School Law 1988*. Albany: New York State School Boards Association, 1988.

Nolte, M. Chester. *How to Survive as a School Board Member: The Legal Dimension.* Chicago: Teach 'em, Inc., 1984.

Rauth, Marilyn. "Exploring Heresy in Collective Bargaining and School Restructuring," *Phi Delta Kappan* 71, no. 10 (1990): 781–784, 788–790.

Reeves, Charles E. *School Boards: Their Status, Functions and Activities*. Westport, Conn.: Greenwood Press, 1954; reprinted 1969.

Reller, Theodore L. *The Development of the City Superintendency of Schools in the United States*. Philadelphia: Theodore L. Reller, 1935.

Reutter, E. Edmund. *The Law of Public Education*, 3d ed. Mineola, N.Y.: Foundation Press, 1985.

Rotunda, R. D.; Nowak, J. E.; and Young, J. N. (1986). *Treatise on Constitutional Law: Substance and Procedures*. St. Paul, Minn.: West Publishing Co., 1986.

Safferstone v. Tucker, 357 S.W. 2d 3 (Ark. 1962).

Schmidt, Peter. "Ohio Lawmakers Sanction Teacher Peer-Review as Fair," *Education Week*, 7 March 1990, p. 14.

State ex rel. Harbach v. Mayor of the City of Milwaukee, 206 N.W. 210 (Wisc. 1925).

State ex rel. Walsh v. Hine, 21 A 1024 (Conn. 1890).

Stuart v. School District Number 1 of the Village of Kalamazoo, 30 Mich. 69 (1874).

Timar, Thomas B. "The Politics of School Restructuring." In *Education Politics for the New Century*, edited by Douglas E. Mitchell and Margaret E. Goertz. New York: Falmer Press, 1990.

Tyack, David B. *The One Best System: A History of American Urban Education*. Cambridge, Mass.: Harvard University Press, 1974.

Walters, Cheryl M., and Wyatt, Terry L. "Toledo's Internship: The Teachers' Role in Excellence," *Phi Delta Kappan* 66, no. 5 (1985): 365–367.

Wiles, Jon, and Bondi, Joseph. *The School Board Primer: A Guide for School Board Members*. Boston: Allyn and Bacon, 1985.

Section II
Love Them or Hate Them: A Debate About the Need for School Boards

CHAPTER 2

Reinventing Local Control

Chester E. Finn, Jr.

So deeply ingrained in our consciousness is the idea of "local control of education" that few Americans even think about it anymore. Like "separation of church and state," "civilian control of the military," and "equality of opportunity," the phrase rolls off the tongue without even engaging the mind. To suggest that it may be obsolete or harmful is like hinting that Mom's apple pie is laced with arsenic.

The time has come, however, to subject "local control" as we know it to closer scrutiny. It is one of those nineteenth-century school governance and finance arrangements that may not serve the country well at the dawn of the next millennium. It is enshrined in neither the Ten Commandments nor the Constitution. It could, therefore, be changed. Indeed, it has already been changing in practice even though we have not yet revamped the theory.

The Constitution, of course, is silent about education. By not being assigned to the federal government, this function was left to the states, and state constitutions are where we find spelled out the duty of the

Reprinted with permission from *Education Week*, January 23, 1991.

commonwealth to furnish education to the citizenry. It is the states that gave themselves this mandate. It is the states that have it today.

Early on, however, all save Hawaii devolved the actual operation of schools to local education agencies. This followed an even older pattern in which towns and villages ran their own schools—or subsidized the work of quasi-private academies serving local children—long before states got into the act. Localities were where most of the public school dollar was raised in those days, too. States set certain rules for schools, to be sure, and as the twentieth century unrolled, they also came to provide additional funds, but it was taken for granted that cities, towns, and counties did the heavy lifting in public education. Though local governance structures varied, the usual pattern involved a lay school committee or board of education that hired a professional superintendent to manage the system.

As might be expected of a fairly stable, mostly rural, and heavily agrarian society sprawled across a continental nation, local school systems were numerous and small. In 1931, there were 128,000 of them, with pupil enrollments averaging just 200. Not until the mid 1950s did their number fall below 50,000. Today, almost 16,000 local districts operate some 83,000 public schools. Many of these "systems" are still tiny, however. In 1988, 55 percent of the districts enrolled fewer than 1,000 students each. (At the other end of the spectrum, 4 percent of the districts, with enrollments greater than 10,000, accounted for nearly half of all students.)

These local-system offices are staffed by more than 200,000 people, and the school boards that direct them comprise about 97,000 individuals.

All this is familiar stuff. The interesting question is whether this legacy of our agrarian past makes sense for our high-tech future. From where I sit, it doesn't. Let me suggest four reasons.

First, states have evolved into the senior partners in school finance. Their portion (now 50 percent) crept past the local share (now 44 percent) in the late 1970s. It continues to rise, and as property-tax-limitation referenda and school-finance-equalization lawsuits proliferate, it seems inevitable that fiscal decisions made in state capitals will increasingly be the decisions that matter most in public education.

Second, states are where most of the action has been with respect to policy innovation, too, as the "excellence movement" took shape in the 1980s and shows no sign of abating in the 1990s. One can cite a handful of exceptions (Rochester, Chelsea [Massachusetts], Chicago) where the main impetus was local, but these pale alongside such statewide reform efforts as those of Kentucky, South Carolina, California, New Jersey, and a dozen other jurisdictions. Moreover, big revisions in high-school graduation requirements, teacher qualifications, and student assessment have been undertaken by virtually every state. Though one can make a case that state activism has actually boosted the policy significance of local school managers too, it's hard to claim that decisions made at the municipal level are even half so important today as they were a decade or two ago. (For a provocative discussion, see Fuhrman and Elmore, 1990).

Third, almost a dozen states have enacted "choice" laws, the underlying principle of which is that youngsters may attend any public school in the state, notwithstanding town or district boundaries, with the state's portion of the money accompanying the pupil in the manner of a virtual public-sector voucher. Several states have also provided for secondary students to take college courses, to reenter different schools than those from which they dropped out, and so forth. State-arranged pupil mobility between city and suburb is part of the racial-desegregation strategy in several jurisdictions as well. The point in all these instances is that children are not obliged to attend the public school where they reside. That means the school board in their place of domicile no longer controls their education unless they want it to.

Fourth, restructuring, decentralization, and school-site management loom large on the education-reform agenda of the 1990s. Yet these are a far cry from what has traditionally been meant by "local control." Today's goal is to confer authority, accountability, and autonomy on the individual school-building staff (and, sometimes, parents), not on a municipal school system. This is the crucial distinction between the sort of reform we see in Chicago today and the kind undertaken in New York City two decades ago. Building-level decision making is a form of local control, of course, but it's not what that term has historically implied.

Similar developments can be spotted across the Atlantic, where British education reformers have conferred sweeping budgetary and personnel authority on individual schools and sharply reduced the powers of local education authorities. (Schools that wish to can even "opt out" of their control altogether and establish a direct relationship with the central government in London.) "The political function of local authorities has become very small," writes Cambridge education professor David Hargreaves, "especially since schools seem free to ignore local policies if they so wish."

What, besides tradition, does "local control" have going for it in American education today? Not even public approbation, it appears from the Gallup education poll. That survey has several times asked respondents whether they would favor national high-school-graduate examinations. By 1988, the proportion endorsing such a drastic departure from customary practice had risen to 73 percent—up from 50 percent in 1958 and 65 percent as recently as 1984. In 1989, Gallup also asked whether people would favor requiring that schools "conform to national achievement standards and goals," "use a standardized national curriculum," and deploy "standardized national testing programs to measure the academic achievement of students." To these, the responses were overwhelmingly affirmative: 70 percent, 69 percent, and 77 percent, respectively, for the public at large, with parents even more favorably disposed (Elam and Gallup, 1989).

How deep-seated could our commitment to "local control" be if two-thirds to three-quarters of the American public are willing to jettison its most important manifestations? Not very, Ernest L. Boyer observed to a newspaper interviewer in early 1990. "I think for the first time America is more preoccupied with national results than local school control," he said. "Today, Hondas and Toyotas and Japanese V.C.R.'s have us really worried about national competitiveness, ..nd that's more important than whether we have local governance. . . . All of this suggests there has been a sea change in the way Americans think about education."

Breathe deeply. What if we were to declare local boards and superintendents to be archaic in the 1990s, living fossils of an earlier age? If one set of important decisions and duties moves up to the state (or even the nation), and another set shifts down to the individual school (and to parents), what is the "local education agency" except another instance of middle management of the sort that most modern organizations are stripping away in the name of efficiency and productivity?

Local school boards are not just superfluous. They are also dysfunctional. They insulate education decisions from voters, taxpayers, and parents. This is ironic, because the theory says they should make schools more responsive to the public. Even though most school boards are elected, however, reality doesn't track theory. The boards have become part of the "establishment." They participate in the peculiar politics of an arena occupied by the suppliers of education services—the employees and managers of the system, the vendors who sell it things, the interest groups that play upon it—rather than the consumers of those services or the taxpayers who underwrite them. That is why the Boston City Council recently moved to abolish that city's school committee and have the schools run from City Hall. The separate governance system wasn't working; the educational needs of Boston's children were not being met. Why cling to an arrangement that isn't getting the job done?

What is more, at a time when radical alterations are needed throughout elementary-secondary education, school boards have become defenders of the status quo. Their members display the same rosy-tinted complacency as do the administrators they hire. Why make big changes in something you think is working O.K. as it is?

Emily Feistritzer's (1989) survey of school board presidents tells us that although they, like the general public, gave low marks to American public education as a whole, four out of five of them awarded grades of A or B to the public schools in their own communities, that is, to the schools over which they have policy oversight. This was not quite so high as the marks conferred by principals and superintendents, to be sure, but it was twice as large a proportion of honors grades as the American people were prepared to give their local schools.

We need change agents in charge of those schools, not preservers of entrenched interests and encrusted practices. If the states discharge their part of the job satisfactorily, specifying the "ends" of education, furnishing resources, and managing the information feedback and accountability systems; if responsibility and authority over the "means" are devolved to the school-building level; and if parents are encouraged to pick any school in the state that, in their judgment, will work well for Matt or Jessica, we could readily dispense with the extra layer.

Local control is dead. Long live local control.

REFERENCES

Elam, Stanley M., and Gallup, Alec M. "The 21st Annual Gallup Poll of the Public's Attitudes toward the Public Schools," *Phi Delta Kappan* 71, no. 1 (1989): 41–56.

Feistritzer, C. Emily. *Profile of School Board Presidents in the U.S.* Washington, D.C.: National Center for Education Information, 1989.

Fuhrman, Susan H., and Elmore, Richard F. "Understanding Local Control in the Wake of State Education Reform," *Educational Evaluation and Policy Analysis* 12, no. 1 (1990): 82–96.

CHAPTER 3

Local Control and "Organizacrats"

Thomas A. Shannon

"We have met the enemy, and they is us !" That's the Pogolike characterization sketched in "Reinventing Local Control" by Chester E. Finn, Jr. Mr. Finn contends, in effect, that people cannot be trusted to govern their own community's public schools.

Democratic representative governance of the public elementary and secondary schools in the local community—as epitomized by the locally elected school board—is old-fashioned and doesn't work anymore, Mr. Finn claims. What's worse, malevolently shoring up every obstacle to education change, he says, are the local school board and its superintendent, both of whom he accuses of being "preservers of entrenched interests and encrusted practices."

Mr. Finn's formula for education improvement: Do away with the local school board, which he excoriates as being "superfluous" and "dysfunctional," and while you're at it, fire the superintendent. Both are "living fossils of an earlier age," he concludes. And because the

Reprinted with permission from *Education Week*, February 13, 1991.

people of an entire community cannot govern their public schools, make each school an island unto its own, connected only with the fatherly authorities in the education bureaucracy in the state capital.

What is Mr. Finn's case for such a radical move? He offers four reasons. Each one is off the mark, and taken as a group, they nullify each other.

His first reason is that states, not local school districts, have evolved over the years as the "senior partners in school finance." To begin with, this general statement has no application to many of the nation's more than fifteen thousand local districts where so-called state aid pays the minority share of financing schools. But, even in those states that have instituted a state equalization formula that has as its base not the wealth of a particular district but the resources of the state as a whole to pay for education, the questions arise: "So what? What bearing does that have on who should govern each community's schools?"

The answer: It has no bearing at all. Regardless of how money comes back to support local school districts, it all begins as tax dollars from each local community. Newer state school-finance formulas— instituted primarily by judicial fiat because the courts found that some states' school-aid-equalization formulas never really equalized resources—have not lowered the tax money that local communities pay for their schools. The state formula merely has changed how such tax money is collected from the local community.

For decades, local school boards have urged state legislatures to use their authority over broader, more flexible tax-revenue sources than the real-property tax available to boards for funding the schools. At no time during years of debate did proponents of an expanded tax base for schools—in local communities or in state legislatures—ever suggest that a good reason to do it was to increase control of the public schools from state capitals. Had they done so, they would have been laughed off the stage.

A logical extension of Mr. Finn's argument would be that, if the federal government ever carries through with the Jeffersonian compact President Bush and the nation's governors signed in Charlottesville, Virginia, in 1989, primary control over education should pass from the states to the federal government. In that agreement are provisions calling for more federal aid to education, as well as a superequalization effort to bring additional federal funding to less affluent states.

Mr. Finn's second argument is even more specious than linking tax-revenue allocation (without regard to source) to school control. It declares that state governments are "where most of the action has been with respect to policy innovation."

This assertion prompts the retort of the old Brooklyn Dodgers fan: "Sez who?!" Education innovation in local districts across the United States during the past decade has been substantial. All it takes is for somebody to notice it. And, aye, there's the rub.

It's not easy for the national media to track innovation in more than fifteen thousand local communities. But, anybody who takes the time to ask the question of local school board members, administrators, or teachers: "How has your instructional program changed in, say, the past five or ten years?" will get an earful.

Certainly state legislatures and governors have enacted considerable school-reform legislation in the past several years, and much of it has advanced the cause of school improvement, especially where proper funding also was included. But most of the specific programmatic ideas that found their way into new state laws and state school board regulations were based on experiences in the local school districts. They did not miraculously appear as visions from heaven in the minds of state education people while out fasting in the desert.

And this is understandable because the best innovators—the most highly qualified teachers and the most able administrators—are employed in local community school systems. It is at the local level that educators are best rewarded, both physically from their professional contribution and financially from better salary schedules than are available at the state level.

As to the other aspects of what advocates call the "education-reform agenda," such as extending the school day and year, conducting year-round school, and substantially raising teacher salaries, school boards know these attractive proposals, as a practical matter, cost big dollars. School districts, board members know, are labor-intensive enterprises. Salary and fringe benefits account for 85 percent of most districts' operating budgets. When people talk about "new programs," they're invariably talking about hiring new people. And when they talk retrenchment, they really mean reducing the number of employees.

The two—employees and programs—are inextricably linked. And that linkage is the basis for the "opposition" school boards and administrators often raise to reform schemes that are either unfunded or woefully underfunded. In return, these tough-decision makers at the local level are pilloried as troglodytes resisting change. But school boards are gatekeepers of reality. And one of the realities school boards and their superintendents always face is matching the available dollars to the myriad proposals that regularly come before them.

It is elemental that reform in schooling occurs only in schools. What many observers count as reform at the state level is actually rhetoric about reform. State legislatures have in fact adopted many oppressive statutes over the years that ruin the type of local school environment needed for innovation. As barnacles slow down ships, these laws that limit school-board discretionary authority over personnel, curriculum, and other crucial operating areas—and that substitute micromanagement by statute—hinder local initiative and stifle local imagination by undercutting boards' authority to act as local policymakers.

Mr. Finn's profferring of the "choice" idea as an argument to abolish local community control of the schools is perhaps the least relevant of all. Local boards generally have no problem with "choice," in which parents select the public school for their children within their district or where state law contemplates cross-district transfer, at least not so long as certain sensible conditions are met: selections must be made for a full school year; racial balance may not be lessened; rules regarding athletic-program eligibility may not be subverted; district transportation costs may not be increased, and so on.

But where "choice" is an excuse to fund private education from public tax money, the opposition is, of course, spirited. Nevertheless, the commonsense fact—buttressed by clear experience in states having cross-district "choice" plans in operation where the number of parents wanting their children to attend schools away from their home area is negligible—is that almost all children will attend school in their own community. It is a mystery how "choice" constitutes a reason to eliminate community control of the public schools, as Mr. Finn asserts.

The final reason he invokes for throwing out local community school boards and their superintendents is a sort of potpourri in which he alleges that everything generally described as educational "restructuring," "decentralization," and "site management" constitutes a triangle sounding the death knell for local community representative governance of its schools. As evidence, he submits the English school governance experience, which is as unlike the United States' experience with local school boards as Parliament and the monarchy are different from Capitol Hill and the White House.

Each local community needs policy control over its schools because they are a community, in fact and at law. The most extreme restructuring plans extant—those of Kentucky and Chicago—recognize this essential sociological and political fact of life by maintaining the local school board with substantial authority over each community's education destiny. The state legislators who advanced those plans know that without the balance provided by a local school board, education would break down into a system of separated school fiefdoms.

This school balkanization of a community would create the kind of "have" and "have not" schools within a community that the *Serrano* line of "equal protection" court cases prohibited among communities within a state. We then would have a worse social-class problem than the one Britain now is trying to shake off. Separate public schools for the very poor, for the middle class, and for the affluent would be the natural result.

The fact is that the public schools in the United States (and Canada) have been decentralized from the start—indeed, too decentralized in light of today's standards and transportation conditions. That's the reason school districts gradually combined or unified over the years so that today, instead of having 128,000 boards, as was the situation in 1930, we have about 15,350. Our challenge is not to go backward toward the extreme decentralization of years long gone but to make the current decentralized community approach to education work.

Local school board governance consists of several indispensable functions. The board translates federal law and integrates state mandates into local policy action; tests proposed educational initiative against the backdrop of community need and sentiment; evaluates on behalf of the entire community the educational program; monitors the work of the superintendent and administrative staff who implement board policy; serves as the final appellate body short of the court system on appeals of citizens and school employees concerning administrative decisions; cooperatively deals (both as a board and as individual board members) with citizens in school matters in the tradition of responsive, responsible representative governance; and interacts with federal, state, and other local-government entities to ensure that the schools are given the attention they deserve.

Each of these functions is so critical that they have given rise to the rubric, "If community school boards didn't exist, we would have to invent them."

School-site management is another phony issue thrown in by Mr. Finn. It is more a case of management style than of basic governance change. Indeed, site management—with its implicit transfer of much administrative authority from the central office to the school site—is related more to how superintendents and principals do their work than how local boards govern education in communities. The abiding concerns of school boards with respect to site management are in reserving to the people of any community, through representative governance, the right to make overall education policy for the community.

And that brings us to another major flaw in Mr. Finn's reasoning: It is naive. Although he presents no coherent plan to govern schools once the school board and superintendent are assigned to perdition, he apparently thinks that individual schools, with vaguely structured, leaderless committees of teachers and parents, can both function effectively and be equal partners with the faraway state bureaucracy. Not only would they foment a kind of neo-anarchy, but they also would be torn asunder by state bureaucracies asserting their "superior" knowledge of what is really best for schools, as they so often do today with local districts serving politically powerful communities.

But Mr. Finn's errant proposal is no surprise. It flows naturally from experience with the U.S. Education Department in a time when advancing specific education ideologies counted more than assessing reality. He is an exemplar of a new breed of education activists most accurately called "organizacrats." Their solution to every problem is, you guessed it: Reorganize! Nobody except an organizacrat would tell reasonable people that they can solve all of their problems by simply reorganizing, and nobody else could do it with a glibness and chutzpah that astounds experienced practitioners.

But, the real or apocryphal wisdom of the ages on the limits of reorganizing is summed up in the injunction of one of the Roman Emperor Nero's deputies, Petronius Arbiter, who declared, "We tend to meet any new situation by reorganizing; and a wonderful method it can be for creating the illusion of progress while producing confusion, inefficiency, and demoralization."

Experienced practitioners of public school governance, administration, and teaching know that the real problems of the schools are a reflection of our society. Schools are not the whole cause of the problems but rather are the places where the problems are most evident in each community.

A holistic approach to enhancing children's natural capacity and desire to learn—one that incorporates concerted action by government, business, labor, churches, and families, as well as the schools—

must be complemented with a public commitment for a sensible dollar investment in children and a resolve to use technology effectively in education.

But, on all three counts—gearing up local communities to address the human dimension of learning, recognizing that true educational change has its roots in societal change and definitely will be no free lunch, and incorporating technology into the curriculum as well as the administration of schools—the record of the U.S. Education Department is a cipher.

It is precisely in these areas, however, that school boards are beginning to guide their districts. That is the genius of the American system of local community governance. And the shame is that it is being done without assistance from Mr. Finn and the other organizacrats so preoccupied with pondering the wrong questions.

Section III
Urban Problems and State Pressures on School Boards

CHAPTER 4

Reallocating the Power of Urban School Boards

Joseph M. Cronin

What can be done to city school boards to stimulate higher educational productivity and to break up the allegedly ineffective bureaucracies that stifle change and improvement? Can boards reform the schools by themselves, or must they seek new allies such as parents and professionals at the school-site level or from higher education?

Every decade of the twentieth century witnessed citizen and legislative crusades to redesign urban school governance, to centralize or decentralize, to switch from appointive to elective boards, to shrink or enlarge the central board, or to recognize or diminish the mayor's role. At the end of the 1980s, two cities tried even more drastic remedies. Chicago took appointment of principals away from the central board of education and gave new duties, control, authority, and money to local school building councils of parents and teachers. Chelsea, Massachusetts, asked Boston University, a major private higher education institution, to take over the management of its low-income, low-performance city school system.

Not everyone cheered these changes. Employee unions, especially of school administrators, were concerned about their rights. Chelsea's

Hispanic parents called for safeguards to protect their children. Intellectuals wondered whether universities had any right to take over a public school system. Many wondered whether Chicago was doomed to experience the same disillusion that followed efforts to expand community control over subunits of the New York and Detroit schools in the 1970s and 1980s.

It must be noted that from the 1890s on, a strong central city board of education and a powerful superintendency were reforms vigorously supported by civic leaders, business executives, university presidents, and other advocates of good government. A much smaller group from time to time advocated the abolition of city school boards and fusion with either general-purpose city government or the creation of a metropolitan or urban county school district such as prevails in many southern states (Cronin, 1973). During the nineteenth century, many cities copied the rural school committee model and appointed school trustees, inspectors, or committees for each school. Often city schools were organized by ward, which at one time was considered a manageable and respectable subunit of the city. Overwhelmed in the 1890s by immigration and poverty, city governance broke down and the educated elites in their wisdom created central bureaucracies to restore order, decency, and—they thought—productivity.

Urban school reform for much of the twentieth century had three purposes:

1. To protect the city school from patronage, bribery (e.g., by textbook suppliers), and other irregularities in administrative promotion and business management. Ward politicians and mayors from time to time treated urban schools the same way they might treat sewer and trolley contracts—as sources of jobs for supporters and wealth in the form of kickbacks.

2. To fix responsibility for employment and for purchasing on a relatively small, easily observed board of incorruptible citizens who should hire top educational executive talent on an impersonal merit system.

3. To assimilate immigrant children into the norms and work ethic of prior generations, using the schools as the major tool of socialization and social control.

During the 1960s and 1970s, minority leaders did not like what they saw. The education of their children was determined by Caucasians, and teachers had been hired years before ostensibly under merit systems and were preserved by tenure systems so strong as to keep out young teachers of other races. Nowhere was this tension more evident or better publicized than in New York. Also, central bureaucracies and boards often failed to prevent political patronage and payroll padding in big city school systems. Before examining recent reform efforts in Chicago or Chelsea, I will review the struggles of New York City and Detroit with earlier versions of school governance reforms. The urban school reforms of the 1990s must be clearly differentiated from the flawed models of yesteryear. A recent Rand Corporation study on educational reform is instructive as we begin this review.

OTHER BIG CITIES: THE BEST OF THE REST

The McDonnell Foundation of St. Louis asked the Rand Corporation to find big cities that were making educational improvements and were winning support from citizens, corporations, and teacher unions. Thirty cities were nominated and six were selected for study: Pittsburgh, Cincinnati, Atlanta, Miami, Memphis, and San Diego. The Rand report, *Educational Progress: Cities Mobilize to Improve Their Schools* (Hill, Wise, and Shapiro, 1989), evaluated the roles of city school boards, superintendents, civic and union leaders, and the sources of initiatives and of funds. The research team looked for change strategies and school improvement models that worked. Each of the cities faced serious problems of inadequate finance, declining student achievement, high dropout rates, and employee strikes.

What these cities shared was a united community commitment to improvement. The key element was the development of a comprehensive school improvement strategy with support from the business community, civic leaders, and labor unions including the organized teachers. The superintendent was the key actor needed to create and explain the mandate for change. There was usually an external community strategy and an inside strategy for the staff, with goals very explicit and information readily available about each school and its performance. What do the school boards do in the more effective cities? First, they select the superintendent and support him or her. Then they must remain united behind a plan and the management. If they argue a great deal of the time or try to micromanage the schools, they will tie down the superintendent and divert resources from implementing the improvements.

Rand's conclusions about urban school boards are modest, even humbling. The main contribution of an urban school board was simply to set a few priorities clearly and select an outstanding educator as superintendent, one who could explain and promote educational improvement both within the community and within the school system by providing symbolic leadership. The Rand report stated:

> In most cities, the board has been a player in someone else's leadership strategy. Board consensus on goals is indispensable. But in most cities, this consensus was created by forces outside the board, by the superintendent, . . . or by business and civic elites that included the board in a communitywide strategy-building process. [P. 27]

With the exception of one or two individual school board members, "school boards seldom invented or motivated the school improvement efforts" (p. 27). The better boards "let the community leadership into the school's business" (p. 28) and supported the priorities agreed to with civic, union, and corporate leadership.

The Rand study reported no clear preference for any one type of urban school board, appointed or elected. Nor was there any finding that "choice" among schools was a key component, although several cities had magnet schools to assist racial integration. The study commended efforts "to return the schools to the unified control of the principal" (p. 44) rather than require submission of reports to multiple central office administrators.

Board conflict or micromanagement or insistence on frequent evening board meetings can, Rand researchers concluded, actually reduce the superintendent's capacity or time available for community leadership. Rand found it useful in Cincinnati and San Diego that board members were willing to lay aside their sovereignty in school issues to work as experts in community problem-solving groups with business, union, university, and other civic leaders to mobilize new support for public education. Neither external grants nor state "choice" plans provided the glue; the Rand "double helix of school reform" was the outside mobilization of political and business support along with the inside stimulation of comprehensive school improvement. Two of the six cities were encouraging more discretion for principals in school management; four were promoting mastery learning, related staff development, and test-based accountability. Both strands are not only important but indispensable.

Rand concluded that "a long-term solution to the problem of any big city's schools will take many years, far longer than the tenure of any superintendent or board" (p. 23). To succeed in the long run, a school improvement plan must provide for its own continuation. A permanent link to community leadership based on such enduring institutions as major locally based corporations and civic groups is essential. Rand's researchers conceded that megalopolises such as Chicago, New York, and Los Angeles will need an extremely high level of sustained political and economic effort to succeed even after a positive start.

NEW YORK CITY

The Ford Foundation under McGeorge Bundy supported New York City Mayor John V. Lindsay's efforts in 1967 to find ways to reform the public schools and accommodate demands of minority parents for a voice in schools that would not or could not be racially integrated (Mayor's Advisory Panel, 1967). In a real sense, "community control" became an alternative to racial desegregation or integration, a constitutionally correct but unpopular remedy in most northern cities. Many cities exploded with racial tension, and power-sharing experiments were financed to relieve some of that tension.

New York City schools in the 1960s already had local advisory boards, but they held virtually no power except to listen and pass on complaints. Three New York City public schools were awarded Ford grants to plan and design community-controlled schools. At the mayor's request, Bundy chaired a panel to advise the city and state on how best to govern the schools. The Bundy panel recommended creating from thirty to sixty school boards to govern all schools in a geographical area, each to hire the teachers and administrators and to try to achieve racial integration. Thirty boards would control thirty thousand pupils each while sixty would have fifteen thousand pupils. Critics worried that extremists could capture the smaller units. Also, the excellence of certain citywide high schools might be jeopardized; therefore the mayor decided that senior high schools should remain under the central board.

Controversy erupted when one of the Ford pilot school boards in mostly minority Ocean Hill-Brownsville (Brooklyn) terminated six Caucasian administrators and thirteen teachers. The unions went out on strike three times in 1968. During 1969, the New York legislature, after much debate, authorized thirty community school districts with elected boards, each of which was to select a community superintendent. However, explicit veto power over textbooks, budgets, and school sites was reserved for a citywide school chancellor and a board of seven, with one member from each borough and two appointed by the mayor. School employees, under the new law, would be protected from arbitrary removal.

For a while, the New York City school decentralization plan seemed to work. Elections were held, experimental programs were launched, and in-service programs were devised by the teachers themselves. The early criticisms were that election turnout was quite low, that not enough blacks and Puerto Ricans were elected, and that boards could fire only the district superintendent rather than all the ineffective educators in a district. Marilyn Gittell, then a New York City university professor, reported that there was substantial progress in minority employment and that in the decade 1969–1979 the proportion of black and Hispanic principals rose from 6 percent to 25 percent and the number of minority district superintendents rose from zero to eight (Gittell, 1980). More than one hundred local school board members, almost one third, were from minorities in a system where between 1955 and 1975 the minority student population had grown rapidly from 28 to 68 percent. However, the voter turnout, which was 15 percent in 1970, fell to 10 percent in 1980, which meant that local political organizations or school employee campaign efforts could influence an election rather easily. The elections cost the city $5 million to run every three years.

Moreover, ordinary parents did not really gain much control over the new boards. A New York City Charter revision study found that the United Federation of Teachers grew very active in supporting candidates for community school boards. "By 1973, 54 percent of those who were elected to local school boards in the city were UFT candidates. The union spent an estimated $127,000 on election-related activity during that year" (Charter Revision Commission for New York City, 1974, p. 66). Ten years later, the union elected a majority of New York City local school board members, demonstrating that "institutional restructuring does not significantly alter the power structure in a community; it merely reshapes the arena in which the truly powerful exercise their influence" (p. 77).

A *New York Times* poll in 1980 found New York city school principals essentially unhappy, with 52 percent of them in favor of decentralization, 10 percent for further decentralization, and 7 percent in favor of a borough system. Only 11 percent of those responding (366 principals) would keep the present system. The *Times* noted that decentralization carried with it daily political pressures on principals and took time away from more important functions such as classroom supervision. "Citing what they said were millions of dollars in unnecessary operating costs, inefficient management techniques, political intrigue, and administrative incompetence, they (principals) said that as bad as they believed the centralized school system was years ago, the decentralized system that replaced it was worse" (*New York Times*, 25 June 1980).

Between 1970 and 1980, six of the thirty-two local boards were charged with corruption. Three school board members in District 5, Harlem, were convicted of conspiracy to misuse public funds in an election campaign. In District 23, Ocean Hill-Brownsville, a school board president was convicted for asking for a bribe from an educational materials vendor. These were precisely the types of activities that in the 1890s led to the clamor for a strong central board. The trade-off for increased citizen participation may be some diversion of funds to less than noble educational purposes.

The corruption continued well into the 1980s. New York state created a special commission to study integrity in the public schools. One district superintendent, Colman Genn of Queens, wore a concealed tape recorder to collect evidence to indict school board members who had three teachers transferred to nonteaching assignments as political favors. Genn testified that he "had forty unnecessary paraprofessionals, most of them friends or political workers for school board members" (*New York Times*, 19 July 1990, pp. A1, B4). Two Brooklyn district superintendents testified that they had a total of 150 unnecessary paraprofessionals. New York City, with 65,000 teachers for 940,000 students, also had 54,000 nonteaching employees—administrators, counselors, security guards, aides, cooks, and others. Local boards could have their budget cut by the central board and chancellor, but could not be told which positions to cut. Investigators visiting seventeen schools in the southwest Bronx found that eighty computers were missing. The same district provided $17,000 so that sixty-eight officials could have beepers, of which forty were given to relatives and friends with no reimbursement to the school. Another district superintendent spent $10,000 of special education funds to redecorate an office. These diversions of school funds represented an unanticipated surcharge on the effort to decentralize the bureaucracy and expand the potential of democracy (*Washington Monthly*, 1990).

Did the decentralization effort take the place of school desegregation in the city? Joseph Viteritti noted that "community school districts have been among the most blatant perpetrators of intentional or de jure segregation in New York. . . . (Some of the boards) are insensitive and unresponsive to the demands of the minority community (Viteritti, 1983).

New York City survived twenty years of decentralization experience that can inform Chicago and other cities. In 1990, New York hired a new school superintendent, Joseph Fernandez from Miami-Dade County. In his position there, he was a superior advocate of school-based management. Fernandez invited New York City schools to submit proposals for educational "power-sharing" among teachers, parents, and principals. This experiment is supported by the United Federation of Teachers, partly because a majority of each school's governing committee will be made up of teachers and other professionals. New York principals and their union, the Council of Supervisors and Administrators, have expressed a need to have veto power over all decisions.

In 1991, eighty New York City public schools (all levels) decided to "share the power" in hiring new teachers and administrators, determining curriculum and work schedules, and making budgets. Twenty-seven of them are high schools and five of them special education schools. Fernandez predicted that, as in Dade County, as many as half of the schools will eventually switch to this mode. Fernandez, however, cannot mandate school-based management, but he has offered to give $20,000 per school for planning activities including conferences and planning retreats. Each school can organize a governing board, which must include the principal, a parent representative, and the school union chairman, and it must also include a majority of nonsupervisory professionals. Key local school decisions would be ratified by parents and faculty. Schools can ask for waivers from union contract provisions and central office regulations if they need flexibility, for example, in revising the school's hours or in making other structural changes.

It will become clear that New York City school "power sharing" will in certain ways resemble what Chicago schools will be like in the 1990s. What is not clear at present is whether Chicago, so long a city recognized for patronage politics, will overcome strong local temptations to exploit school jobs and contacts for personal or partisan gain.

THE DETROIT EXPERIENCE

While New York City was experimenting with community control, Detroit schools in 1967 established regions of thirty thousand pupils, each led by a regional superintendent. In 1969, State Senator Coleman Young proposed a more dramatic devolution of control to regional boards with broad authority to develop new curricula, hire the regional superintendents, and test the pupils. The Detroit central board would include both regional representatives and some citywide representatives. Another legislative version, calling for eight regional school districts, passed in 1970. However, Detroit soon became embroiled in a major controversy over racial segregation; the integrationist board members were recalled; new school boundaries separated white and black regions; and minority influence actually declined. In short, the Detroit school decentralization plan did not work very well at all.

During the 1980s, a major recession in the automobile industry created serious financial problems for all Michigan schools. Detroit suffered heavily, accumulating a school budget deficit of more than $150 million, and Detroit schools lost a referendum to raise new school taxes. A board election in 1988 attracted four new reform members who called for a dramatic turnaround in the schools and won passage of new taxes. Then in August 1990, the central board agreed to try to "empower" local schools by

1. allowing schools to plan their own programs and select staffs and instructional strategies;
2. seeking to obtain waivers from state rules or union contract provisions;
3. applying for empowerment status (if approved by 75 percent of teachers and 55 percent of parents, noninstructional staff, and students);
4. designing their own staff development plan and school schedules;
5. seeking and spending $5,000 per school to be used as the school sees fit (National School Boards Association, 1990).

All 272 schools in the district presumably will be "empowered" by 1994 with discretion over decisions to allocate $5,000 per school or $10 per pupil. Such a sum, of course, is but a minuscule share of the funds spent on each pupil. However, an empowered staff could seek additional budget and contractual authority from the central staff.

The 1990 interim superintendent was Dr. John Porter, dynamic former Michigan State Superintendent of Instruction and former Chairman of the College Board. In 1991, the board searched for a new superintendent. Thus, Detroit emerges from the financial and governance crisis of earlier decades to design, under new leadership, a modest local school empowerment program. How does this compare to Chicago?

CHICAGO SCHOOLS

In response to the publication of *A Nation at Risk* in 1983 and other reports, the Illinois General Assembly in 1985 enacted major school reform legislation after thorough study of Illinois priorities and a major debate over what should be done. Early childhood education, increased student testing and local school accountability, and dozens of other specific reforms were signed into law by Governor James Thompson.

The almost six hundred Chicago schools appeared not to change much despite this legislation. The *Chicago Tribune* in 1987 assigned fourteen reporters and more than a dozen photographers and special editors to carry out a thorough study of Chicago schools. After seven months of visits and interviews and tours of eight other cities, the *Tribune* dropped a bomb—two weeks of daily criticism of every aspect of Chicago schools (the teaching, the supervision, the central bureaucracy, the unions) followed by a major editorial recommendation for a "big scale voucher system." (*Chicago Tribune*, 15–29 May 1988.)

Actually, the Chicago business community and the Chicago minority community had been concerned about the shortcomings of Chicago public schools for many years. A critical incident occurred in 1980. The Chicago banks became nervous about combined threats by state and federal officials to cut off financial support for an illegally segregated school system. When notified by Moody's investment rating service about illegal use of restricted funds for operating costs, the banks cut off new credit for cash-poor Chicago schools and refused to lend any more money for the schools. The ensuing financial crisis led to a full-scale legislative review of a school system overextended financially and to a new School Finance Authority, a review panel designed to keep Chicago schools under tight financial and budgetary controls during the 1980s and beyond (Cronin, 1981).

This chapter does not chronicle the complete history of Chicago school reform during the 1980s. However, it is important to note that many groups—such as business professionals, minorities, and university professors—created a steady drumbeat of support for drastic Chicago school reform during the 1980s. Donald Moore (1989) has written a full account summarizing the mounting pressure for reform.

One of the few groups that combined black and white leaders was a coalition created in 1973 called Chicago United, steered by a large executive committee of minority and Caucasian business executives committed to racial accord and to equal opportunity. The unifying cause célèbre for this group was the deficiencies of Chicago schools and their graduates. Chicago United published a series of reports during the 1980s.

In 1981, their special task force on education surveyed the Chicago public schools and called for raising the importance of the role of the principal in the Chicago schools; establishing measurable goals and performance objectives; developing an annual plan to achieve board objectives; and restructuring the central office (Chicago United, 1981). Chicago United found the existing multilayered bureaucracy ineffective and planning nonexistent. However, the 1981 report with its 253 recommendations led to very little response or action.

In 1983, Chicago United published "Agenda for Public Education," highlighting five areas for action: the education program, the teaching staff, community involvement, systemwide leadership, and inadequate funding for education. The report also recommended parent councils for each school, improved school-to-work transitions, and a new formula for state aid to schools (Chicago United, 1983).

During 1984–1985, Chicago United, the Roosevelt University Center for American Policy Studies, and the Illinois Program for School Reform prepared a report entitled *Education for a New Illinois: The Public Schools in a Changing Economy* (Chicago United and Roosevelt University, 1985). Subsequent state reform legislation authorized some funding for local school councils and required semiannual reports from the councils to be submitted to a legislative panel.

In 1987, Chicago United published a reassessment of its 1981 report and urged decentralization of Chicago public schools; more authority for school principals; local school councils with power to make budgets and plans and power to hire and fire principals; and systematic efforts to improve achievements in reading and mathematics (Chicago United, 1987, pp. 16–19).

Another Chicago-based reform oganization, Designs for Change, organized low-income and minority parents to press for spending on special education, programs to reduce dropouts, and programs designed to promote improvement at the school level. As early as 1986, Designs for Change built a network of parent leaders in forty schools, primarily on Chicago's south side, and decided to promote local school governance and school-level management. Chicago media gave excellent coverage to research reports from Designs for Change.

In October 1988, Mayor Harold Washington convened an educational summit meeting of one thousand persons to promote school reform, but the mayor died shortly after initiating the process. Meanwhile, several business groups had formed the Chicago Partnership, which brought together seven business organizations representing forty-five hundred Chicago area employers, including the Chicago Association of Commerce and Industry, the Civic Committee of the Commercial Club, various economic development and metropolitan planning groups, and Chicago United. The partnership called for "a system that is far more responsive to student needs and far more flexible at the school and community level. Major restructuring of the system must emphasize return of school governance to parents and community, returning authority to the principal and recognition of the paramount importance of the teacher and support of the teacher's work" (Mitchner, 1989, p. 32). The partnership wanted local school improvement councils to have governance power. It also called for more student and parental choice and a reduced central office.

The business community was only one source of support for major change, but it was a source that the Republican governor of Illinois (1977–1991) and a majority of downstate Illinois legislators found credible. Support came from many *Fortune 500* companies, the major utilities, steel companies, manufacturers, retail stores, and insurance companies that along with agriculture interests fueled the Illinois economy. The repeated cries of alarm about Chicago schools and the increasingly specific reform plan caught the attention of Chicago representatives to the state legislature.

Chicago Democrats also listen to corporate executives. One legacy of Mayor Richard J. Daley was that corporate, union, and city leaders worked together to achieve political consensus whenever possible. Usually, major education policy proposals were moderated by urban political leaders, but in the 1980s, the business leaders made proposals for school reform that resembled those of (1) intellectuals, social service providers, and university professors who had also been calling for a radical restructuring of Chicago schools; (2) minority group leaders, frustrated by mediocre results, who themselves had proposed major changes; and (3) the menu of changes for Chicago school governance recommended by the Illinois State Board of Education.

Between 1986 and 1988, a new coalition of school reform groups formed Chicago United to Reform Education (CURE), advocating replacing tenure for principals with a multiyear performance contract negotiated with an elected parent-teacher school council. The CURE group filed a comprehensive Chicago school reform bill in 1988, and the business leaders joined with community activists in financing a major public relations campaign to lobby for its implementation.

The issues of Chicago school reform were resolved at the state level. The Chicago School Reform Act, which was passed by the Illinois General Assembly on December 1, 1988, carried out the spirit of the following reform recommendations:

1. Each Chicago public school would be governed by a local school council (LSC), which would select the principal, approve a school improvement budget plan, and evaluate the performance of professionals in carrying out a school plan.
2. Each council would include six parents elected by other parents, two community residents elected by the community, and two teachers elected by the other teachers.
3. The principal must be selected unanimously by the council for a four-year term; would negotiate a performance-based contract that reflects educational goals; would prepare for the council a school improvement plan to increase achievement; would be able to hire and fire all employees and "remediate" teachers for a forty-five-day period or up to one year.
4. Each school would elect a representative to a subdistrict council, which by a 60 percent majority would elect a subdistrict superintendent (SDS) with a four-year performance-based contract. The SDS would monitor school performance, especially for "at-risk" schools.
5. The old Chicago Board of Education was dissolved by state action and replaced by an interim board in May 1989 to serve for one year. Then a new fifteen-member central Board of Education would be recommended by a school board nominating

commission and appointed by the mayor. Its major functions would be the development of a systemwide education reform plan and the selection of a General Superintendent of Schools with a three-year performance-based contract. The board must live within a state-imposed administrative spending cap, although an adjustment waiver could be sought for one year. The board was to approve citywide collective bargaining contracts.

6. The school board nominating commission would consist of one member from each subdistrict council and five chosen by the mayor.
7. Teachers would serve on a Professional Personnel Advisory Committee at each local school to advise the principal and council about curriculum, school improvement, staff development, and budget.
8. The existing Chicago School Finance Authority (created in 1979–1980 to monitor budgets, bonds, and expenditures) would assume a larger watchdog role over the implementation of these reforms.

Each school improvement plan would cover a span of three years. One key goal was student proficiency in mathematics, reading, writing, and higher-order thinking skills to meet or surpass national norms. Other specific goals included attendance levels at or higher than national norms; preparation of students for postsecondary education; preparation for transition from school to work; a decrease in the dropout rate, such as 5 percent each year; and overall school improvement gains each year. Critics of these proposals said that changes in governance would not by themselves bring about school improvement. Missing were funds for early childhood or preschool education, a massive teacher retraining program, computers or technology in the schools, and health and social services programs. However, the corporate and minority coalition held firm for organizational and structural changes that would break the old rigid bureaucracy.

Another strategy for reform written into the Illinois Chicago School Reform Act of 1988 was the expansion of parental choice among public schools. The act mandated development of such a plan for the 1991–92 school year. The case for choice was stated in a publication entitled *We Can Rescue Our Children* (Walberg and Bikalis, 1988). Support for choice also came from the City Club of Chicago, which favored, as had the *Chicago Tribune*, vouchers for low-income school children. During the 1980s, Chicago had developed a magnet school desegregation plan. Approximately half of the one hundred thousand public high school children attend high schools out of their home areas, many going to vocational, technical, or special academic programs. Approximately 20 percent of the elementary school children voluntarily choose a magnet school. A 1990 study by Designs for Change questioned any measurable achievement score gains at magnet schools and asserted that mainly whites and Asians took advantage of choice options (Poinsett, 1990, p. 3).

Both the Chicago Urban League and Leadership for Quality Education (LQE), a corporate school reform group, opposed reliance on choice as a strategy to combat unproductive schools. Others criticized the transportation costs, which at the elementary level already were $31 million. Transportation must be provided free to children of low-income families. The City Club's Edward Marciniak, president of the Institute of Urban Life at Loyola University, urged broadening the choice program to include parochial and private schools. While state superintendent of education, I proposed in 1978 a suburban option for Chicago minorities as well, parallel to what Milwaukee, Hartford, and Boston have done. However, any choice plan must compete with local school councils for scarce state funds for the next five years.

The central office of the Chicago schools, long criticized for excessive overhead costs and bureaucratization, was a major target for reform. The reform law called for a percentage cap on central administrative costs, which had risen to consume more than 30 percent of the total school budget. The "administrative cap" limits spending in noninstructional areas such as building maintenance, security, transportation, food and financial services, research, and staff development. The Illinois statewide average was set at 28.9 percent in 1989 and 27.9 percent in 1990–91. The new general superintendent, Ted Kimbrough, was given a mandate to streamline the central office. He proposed reducing the number of district superintendencies from twenty-three to eleven, with each district office to serve sixty schools. Approximately two hundred members of the central office staff were transferred out of that office to assist the schools and respond to the needs of school councils, principals, and staff. As of 1990, twenty-five hundred people worked at the central office and district centers.

In 1990, Michael Kirst, of Stanford University, was asked to make an interim evaluation of progress. He provided these comments:

Personnel cutbacks came quickly. . . . Entire divisions, such as staff development and curriculum, have been decimated. Some workers retired, others were
scattered among schools. Reform's goal of reducing the size of the central office
has been largely reached. [Kirst, 1990, p. 15]

Kirst found, however, that many central office functions needed
substantial overhaul, especially changes in the form of local school
budgets and in the ways of allocating funds to local schools; instructional leadership and revision of the testing program; and development of reliable performance indicators, such as those provided in San
Diego, Dallas, or Dade County (Kirst, 1990, pp. 17–18).

Chicago schools have begun to provide information on a large
number of indicators—attendance, graduation, achievement on test
scores. Less than a third of Chicago public school students are at or
above norms in reading or mathematics. The high school graduation
rate is 47 percent. Twenty-five percent of high school students failed
at least one course. Several schools have joined Theodore Sizer's
Coalition of Essential Schools, which promotes a much broader array
of evaluations beyond standardized test scores.

Several Chicago foundations helped finance a monthly magazine of
comments on Chicago school reform, critiques, and bulletin board
progress reports on issues and accomplishments. The journal is called
Catalyst and is published by the Community Renewal Society, which
for many years reported on race relations in Chicago. In 1989 and
1990, *Catalyst* included quotations from dozens of teachers, parents,
and others involved. Complaints include too little training for councils, rushed deadlines for negotiating contracts with principals, inadequate help on lump-sum budgeting, antagonism over personnel
decisions, and frustrations over custodial performance and union power.

Mayor Richard M. Daley appointed the fifteen-member school
board to oversee the forty thousand Chicago school workers and the
$3 billion budget. He appointed seven blacks, three Hispanics, three
whites, an Asian American, and an Arab American. The racial mix
represents Chicago's overall population more closely than it represents the school population. *Catalyst* reported that five members came
from the same far South Side district 9, and four from the North Side
district 2, which may reflect where activist nominees live more than
anything else.

Certainly the Chicago school reform bill attracted many candidates
for school councils and increased participation. Almost 10,000 parents
stood for local school council election, as did 2,500 teachers. A total of

312,255 individuals cast votes. The numbers of minority parents elected included 3,200 African Americans and 1,000 Hispanics, similar to the pupil composition of the Chicago schools. As many as 263 businesses and organizations adopted a school (less than half of the schools but still a major increase). Moreover, training was provided for the candidates for local councils (six hours) and for those elected to the councils.

The success of Chicago school reform will not be known for at least four years—the time needed for first-graders to reach grade five and for high school freshmen to graduate or drop out. Four years is also the length of a principal's contract. As of 1994, how many principals will meet their goals, have their contracts renewed, or be fired for failure to perform? Will the system's performance improve? Will public confidence in the Chicago schools improve? Will enough money be made available to support the programs and services needed?

The Chicago Evaluation

On January 1, 1991, the Chicago schools completed one year under the new reform act, much of that time being devoted to planning and transition. Many local and state groups, however, are evaluating progress and reporting on initial accomplishments. Donald Moore (1990) of Designs for Change presented an advocate's perspective:

1. Skeptics argued that not enough persons would run, but 17,256 candidates ran for 5,400 seats on local school councils in October 1989. Ninety-eight percent of the councils had sufficient candidates for every position. Parent turnout in the election was 35 percent for elementary schools and 12 percent for high schools, which compared favorably to 11 percent participation in suburban Cook County school board elections.
2. The racial composition of Chicago school councils was a potential concern. However, 56 percent of parents on local school councils are black, compared with a 59 percent black student population. Twenty-three percent of school council parents are Hispanic, compared with a 26 percent Hispanic student population. Twenty percent are white, compared with a 12 percent white student population.
3. Would they fire all the principals, or keep everyone in their

positions? Of the 256 schools allowed to select a principal, over 82 percent kept the same principals. Approximately fifty retired, declined to apply, sought other positions, or were not reviewed. A dozen schools experienced protests or demonstrations. When the selection process was analyzed, no relationship was found between the racial majority of the council and the race or retention of the principal.

After one year, the Chicago central administration staff was reduced from 3,300 to 2,660, not enough to please all critics but in compliance with the level provided for in the state law. The $40 million in savings was reallocated to the schools along with $89 million in discretionary state funds in 1989–90, and $139 million in 1990–91. Each school received an average of $250,000 in state discretionary funds to spend on specialized teachers, aides, materials, or educational activities. Seven hundred additional teachers and six hundred school counselors and social workers were hired (Moore, 1990).

A polling organization surveyed local school council members in 1990. They asked, "Is your school operating better, worse, or the same as before the election?" Sixty-two percent of teachers and 60 percent of principals said their schools were operating better. Only 6 percent of each group said their schools were worse. Eighty-one percent of parents said schools were operating better, and only 3 percent responded worse. Eighty-five percent of the black parents felt their school was operating better. Parents in general were most pleased with improvements in safety and discipline, parent-staff relations, and planning for the learning process. Even the most difficult areas of physical plant improvements were seen as improved by 52 percent of the principals, 48 percent of the teachers, and 61 percent of the parents (Designs for Change, 1991). Three quarters or more of teachers, principals, and parents felt a sense of optimism that the next school year would be even better. This ends a decade of skepticism and pessimism, even bitter despair as to whether the Chicago schools could ever improve.

The quality of plans for school improvement varied from highly creative to pedestrian. No democratic process can mandate inspiration. One obstacle might be the principal, but observers predict that by 1991–92 the turnover rate for principals may reach 50 percent. Additional principals will retire or leave and the ones who remain will essentially be those who can present a menu of productive ideas to a school council or, better still, can elicit and coordinate ideas flowing from a creative parent, faculty, and community group.

Illinois Bell awarded $10,000 grants to the twenty-six local school councils demonstrating significant progress in planning for and improving their schools. In addition, the company encouraged its employees to run for places on the councils. Thirty-three Illinois Bell employees were elected.

What is so different in Chicago from New York City or Detroit is the decision to focus most of the attention on the local school rather than on a region of twenty-five thousand or more students. Also, parents and citizens have been given genuine authority over selection and retention of the principal, who in turn is given more voice in the selection of new teachers. The stakes are thus higher, which may explain why the 16 percent voter turnout in the council elections exceeds the 11 percent turnout in school board elections in suburban Cook County.

When Chicago principals challenged the new reform act, the Illinois Supreme Court declared the law unconstitutional in November 1990 because it violated the principle of "one man, one vote" in electing members of local school councils. At this writing, stopgap legislation permits the councils to continue operation while the Illinois legislature considers ways of electing council members that will meet the objections of the state Supreme Court.

THE BOSTON UNIVERSITY–CHELSEA AFFILIATION

The Boston University–Chelsea program grew out of two offers (made in 1981 and 1985) by Boston University President John Silber to run the Boston public schools more efficiently and at less cost. When Boston refused these offers, school officials from two other smaller Massachusetts cities, Lowell and Chelsea, asked, "Would you be willing to help us?"

It is important to note that Chelsea is a much poorer city than Boston but is close enough to the central city to be a credible model for reform. Chelsea is an industrial city of twenty-five thousand people, one of the poorest in Massachusetts. The city was best known for a major bridge (the Tobin) connecting Boston with the suburbs north of Boston, for a soldiers' and sailors' retirement home, the abandoned Chelsea naval base, a major produce distribution center, and numerous junkyards. Of the thirty-five hundred students, more than 60 percent come from families on welfare and 55 percent are Hispanic. For 60 percent of the children, English is a second language. The dropout rate is 52 percent each year. Test scores are among the very lowest in the state. The students attend three elementary schools (one is housed in the middle school) and one high school, all with buildings more than eighty years old. No city school system in New England in the 1990s faced more challenges than Chelsea.

As a first step, Boston University agreed to conduct a thorough assessment of the needs of Chelsea schools. In 1988, the Boston University faculty and consultants issued a 350-page plan recommending major changes beginning with preschool classes for three- and four-year-olds, a nutrition program for infants and pregnant women, and a total redesign of educational curricula (Boston University, 1988). Boston University then asked the city to grant the university total management responsibility for the schools. In effect, Boston University would take over the operational duties from the locally elected school committee. The teachers union strongly objected, partly because Boston University had fought and defeated its own faculty union over collective bargaining. The city of Chelsea and Boston University also needed to obtain state legislation to authorize a private university to act as the governing body for a public school system.

Boston University (1988) proposed the following ambitious set of seventeen goals for Chelsea schools:

1. Revitalize the curriculum of the city's school system.
2. Establish programs for the professional development of school personnel and for the expansion of learning opportunities for parents.
3. Improve test scores of students in the school system.
4. Decrease the dropout rate for students in the school system.
5. Increase the average daily student attendance rate for the school system.
6. Increase the number of high school graduates for the school system.
7. Increase the number of high school graduates for the school system that go on to attend four-year colleges.
8. Increase the number of job placements for graduates of the school system.
9. Develop a community school program through which before-school, after-school and summer programs are offered to students in the school system and through which adult education classes are offered to inhabitants of the city.
10. Identify and encourage the utilization of community resources.
11. Establish programs that link the home to the school system.

12. Decrease teacher absenteeism in the school system.
13. Improve the financial management of the school system and expand the range of operating funds available to the school system.
14. Increase salaries and benefits for all staff, including raising the teacher salary average to make it competitive with the statewide average.
15. Construct effective recruiting, hiring, and retention procedures for staff members.
16. Establish student assessment designs and procedures that are of assistance in monitoring programs and that act as incentives for staff members in each school.
17. Seek to expand and modernize physical facilities in the school system.

The Chelsea Teachers Union, the Massachusetts Federation of Teachers, and the American Federation of Teachers (AFT) strongly questioned the Boston University proposal. Albert Shanker, AFT president, raised a series of questions in his weekly *New York Times* column about the privatization of a public school system. Would the university be able to fire existing teachers? How would Boston University treat seniority and promotion rights? Would meetings be open and votes taken? To whom would a private university be accountable? Shanker's criticisms of Boston University were severe. The university could not, he warned, produce either the expertise or the resources needed. It was "making promises that are irresponsible, . . . like going to a doctor who promises to cure your cancer" (Shanker, 1989, pp. 35–37). Although the university asserted that collective bargaining rights would not be abrogated, the AFT filed a lawsuit challenging the Boston University management.

Boston University's plan for Chelsea, "A Model for Excellence in Urban Education," expands substantially the definition of urban education by proposing (1) infant nutrition and special programs for pregnant women and their children until age three; (2) year-round, day-long education and child care every working day; (3) an intergenerational literacy program for non-English-speaking adults as well as for children; (4) a mentoring system for children from single-parent homes; (5) an individualized education plan, moving well beyond the legal requirement that such plans be developed for handicapped children only. The program also called for computers in the classroom. Boston University proposed "minisabbaticals" for teachers to visit other schools and a major emphasis on literacy education and character education in the schools.

The university also called for a massive increase in spending, from both public and private sources. The city itself pleaded a shortage of funds. After 1988, the state was losing revenues and cutting back on virtually all state expenditures, including aid to local schools. During the first year (1989–90), Boston University raised $2.4 million in new funds against a goal of $3 million. Chelsea, meanwhile, faced with a shortfall in state and local revenue, decided to lay off fifty teachers and prepared for a teacher strike because there was no hope of a raise. Boston University allocated $500,000 for a one-time 5 percent salary increase for faculty and agreed to rehire the fifty teachers. The minimum salary was raised from $18,000 to $21,000. The teachers union began to feel that Boston University was supportive of its membership (Greer, 1990).

Hispanic parents were among the most vocal in questioning the offer of the university, in part because they did not feel adequately consulted and possibly because President Silber was critical of bilingual education programs. A group of Hispanic parents filed a lawsuit, asking the state, as had the teachers, to turn down the Boston University plan.

The state legislature approved the plan in 1989, with the provision that the state board of education appoint a panel to monitor programs and safeguard the public interest. The Chelsea Oversight Panel included a Hispanic educator, a former U.S. Commissioner of Education, a former U.S. Secretary of Labor, the chief executive officer of a large Boston law firm, and a black businessman who had served on the State Board of Education. The chairman was a suburban school superintendent who had lived in Chelsea as a youth. This state panel was to advise the state board of any serious problem with the Boston University stewardship of schools, and was to assure public accountability. The superintendent then had to provide information and meet with these and other organizations.

During 1989 and 1990, Chelsea had not one but two boards overseeing the schools. The Boston University management team took charge of school operations, and hired Diana Lam, a Boston zone superintendent, to replace the Chelsea incumbent. The Chelsea School Committee agreed that it would not function as a board but would review all management decisions. It could overrule all but personnel decisions with a two-thirds vote. Moreover, it could cancel the agreement with Boston University by a majority vote at any time.

Although many corporations and foundations contributed to the Boston University–Chelsea project, several major foundations held back resources. As a result, the opening of the early learning center was deferred to a second year. However, Boston University is committed to remain for a ten-year period, provided Chelsea officials continue to want its involvement.

Although the teachers union and Hispanic parents were the early and most vocal critics, Boston University had strong support within Chelsea. One leader was Andrew Quigley, editor of the Chelsea *Record* and former mayor and chairman of the school committee. Another advocate was Richard Voke, Chelsea's state representative, who chaired the powerful House Ways and Means committee. If the state economy rebounds in the 1990s, Voke's support could be critical in further raising state aid both for basic programs and for new school facilities.

Around the country, other university presidents and deans have voiced either interest or skepticism, or have opted to "wait and see." Many say their colleges are not equipped or willing to run an entire urban school system. However, other educators have begun to comment on the Chelsea experiment and programs to date. The *American School Board Journal* praised the comprehensiveness of the Boston University–Chelsea plan, especially its holistic nature. The plan emphasized "the caring, as well as the educational, dimension of elementary and secondary schooling. The focus on the total child— through child care for working parents, early childhood education, good nutrition, schools remaining open after school as community centers for children, values or character education, and the like— constitute an operating plan that is dramatically different from the ordinary. The plan will be monitored closely by school people across the United States" (Shannon, 1989).

Boston University requested the U.S. Department of Education to finance an independent evaluation by Pelavin Associates, a consulting firm based in Washington, D.C., which regularly assists the U.S. Department of Education and other clients on reviews of complex projects.

Boston University released its own progress report to the community, the state, the faculty, and prior and future contributors. The report was prepared by Peter Greer, Dean of the Boston University School of Education, who was formerly U.S. Deputy Undersecretary of Education and at one time the superintendent of schools in Portland, Maine. At various stages, Dean Greer and his management team also involved the colleges of management, arts and sciences, public health, social work, and other faculties at Boston University. He recruited two hundred student volunteers to tutor in Chelsea (Greer, 1990). Dean Greer's report lists several dozen accomplishments, including the formulation of plans, the establishment of councils and workshops, and the convening of meetings. Some of the most dramatic events or actions included the following: (1) the recruitment of the new superintendent, Diana Lam, an experienced Hispanic-Asian American educator; (2) the installation of classroom computers and the computerization of the Chelsea school budget, guidance, and special education systems; and (3) the offer of two full four-year scholarships at Boston University for Chelsea high school students and eight graduate scholarships each semester for Chelsea teachers to improve their professional skills.

The report for 1989–90 acknowledged several areas needing improvement: (1) the search for outside funding was to be contingent on decisions by Chelsea to raise the local tax effort from 17 percent of the municipal budget to more acceptable levels as a "prerequisite for convincing external donors that Chelsea is serious about school reform"; (2) the need for tutors had outrun the supply and the logistics of getting Boston University students to Chelsea needed improvement, such as shuttle van service; and (3) the Chelsea Executive Advisory Committee lacked a clear definition of the relationships among the Chelsea School Committee, the University management team, and the school improvement councils and other parent groups.

Another complicating factor was that three educational experts with important responsibilities in the Chelsea project (Dean Greer, of the School of Education; Theodore Sharp, associate dean and Chelsea project supervisor; and Diana Lam as superintendent) were ultimately accountable to three boards: (1) the Boston University management team, which assumed primary responsibility for the Chelsea schools, for community relations, and for coordination of the many projects initiated by separate faculties at Boston University; (2) the Chelsea School Committee, which continued to hold elections and which retained the right to terminate Boston University's management of the schools at any point, although it had contracted out all operational responsibility to the university; and (3) the Chelsea Oversight Panel appointed by the State Board of Education to monitor the way in which a private university abides by public laws and protects the right of Chelsea citizens and groups for access to the management team and the decision process.

Preliminary Evaluations of the Project

In addition to the university's own progress report, the Chelsea schools were evaluated after "year one" by two external sources: (1) a *Newsweek* (1990) report, and (2) the state's Chelsea Oversight Panel Report issued in November 1990.

For the entire first year of the Boston University–Chelsea experiment, *Newsweek* reporters attended Chelsea school meetings and interviewed participants. On September 17, 1990, the magazine published a journalist's report card and concluded that the experiment was not a "miracle cure." If this is a mess that can be cleaned up by the "can-do men from academia," *Newsweek* observed, "it hasn't happened yet." President Silber's response was, "Don't ask us to show you anything for five years. It took about thirty years to mess up the system. Who says we can correct it in three or four?"

Newsweek praised many of the interim accomplishments: the adult literacy campaign that taught sixty-six adults how to read; the alternative high school programs; the creation of a forty-five-member teacher board and the newsletter for communications; teacher visits to excellent kindergarten and first-grade programs in the Boston area; the new three-year teacher contract with Chelsea's teachers union; and the phasing out of a tracking system that isolated most Hispanic children.

The magazine clearly respected the Boston University decision to establish a preschool program, a pilot early learning center for 154 students that began in September 1990. The full preschool program, which *Newsweek* concluded cost as much as $7 million, remained "a major foundation grant away." The Ford and Rockefeller foundations reportedly found the proposal very costly and therefore difficult to replicate elsewhere. The only discordant report was from Elizabeth McBride, a member of the Chelsea School Committee, who said that Boston University's "involvement in prenatal care, drug abuse, and day care was not understood by Chelsea. A lot of folks here think they are trying to run the city." However, for Chelsea to succeed educationally, it may well need such a comprehensive family services strategy.

The first Latino Chelsea school board member, Marta Rosa, ran in 1990 on a platform opposing Boston University and urging community empowerment as the alternative remedy. But Morris Seigal, also on the board, told the press "for years there's been a malaise over the

Chelsea school system and now things are changing. There is hope where before there wasn't any. We have goals toward which we are moving. . . . We may disagree over how to get there but at least we are heading there. At least somebody is trying" (*Washington Post*, 5 August 1990, p. 11).

In its report of November 20, 1990, the state's Chelsea Oversight Panel (1990) gave the Chelsea project a favorable first-year review with several reservations. The panel emphasized that its role was not to question the educational decisions but to determine whether Boston University was acting in an open, cooperative, and publicly accountable fashion. Panel members conducted hearings and visited Chelsea on four occasions to prepare the report on the first year (1989–90). Commendations flowed for the positive energy and creative spirit of the university team, for the dynamic leadership of Diana Lam, and for the bold structural changes at the high school in curriculum and school business services.

What bothered the panel? Calling the Boston University group the "management team" blurred the distinction between policy and implementation decisions. The panel called for answers to fundamental questions: Who establishes policy for the Chelsea public schools? Are policies established in meetings of the management team? How do the management team, the school committee, and the executive advisory committee relate to each other and to the superintendent? What procedures are to be followed to resolve these questions? The panel also described tensions that persist between Boston University and community constituencies and concluded that "there is not yet the mutual trust and respect needed for long-term success."

The panel mentioned the need for specific educational objectives and evaluation strategies. They also concluded that a university alone cannot raise all the money needed in Chelsea and that the early assumptions about new external funds were unduly optimistic. The final recommendation was to extend the reach of the Boston University–Chelsea project to include economic development and adequate public funding for public education if the handicaps of poverty are to be overcome.

The Chelsea superintendent of schools arranged for a survey of public school parents to assess their concerns and attitudes (Institute for Responsive Education, 1990). At the end of the first year, 70 percent of the parents responding gave the school system A or B and only 2 percent gave the schools a failing grade. The parents listed safety as the number one factor in choosing a school, more important to them even than the curriculum or the school's reputation. Chelsea parents wanted drug and alcohol education programs, summer youth programs, instruction in English as a second language (for immigrant children), and the teaching of moral values such as respect for property and for others. Large numbers of parents wanted instruction in additional languages. Half of the families had used Chelsea schools for less than five years. Twenty-five percent were from Puerto Rico. Forty-three percent spoke Spanish, 10 percent spoke Khmer, and 4.4 percent spoke Vietnamese as a first language. The survey revealed that fewer than half of the parents had graduated from high school, and 6 percent had completed college. Many students entered school after first grade, a phenomenon that reflects the mobility of immigrant families. In spite of some criticism of the survey, Boston University quietly defended the instrument used and the use of the results to generate external support from corporations, foundations, and government and to help prioritize the educational offerings.

URBAN SCHOOL REFORM: SOME POSITIVE AND NEGATIVE PERSPECTIVES

Even within the first two years of the 1990s, it is possible to construct a balance sheet of credits and debits for these new reform initiatives. The possible advantages include the following:

1. Universities are potentially great partners for, and supporters of, schools. American education is flawed by the arbitrary dividing line that separates the high schools from higher education after grade twelve. One's intellectual development as a citizen and worker should be continuous and not reliant on public enthusiasm for the university level and skepticism or scorn for the schools. David Manasian (1990) wrote about California: "The state's large, publicly financed university system is still excellent. But the deterioration in California's primary and secondary schools has caused concern for years . . . and has alarmed its largest employers." Japanese education is considered superior at the elementary and secondary levels, less than impressive at the university level—essentially the reverse of California and much of the United States.

If this is true, then state universities and the stronger private universities could play an important role in strengthening what were once called the common schools. Harvard's James B. Conant spent considerable time, both as university president and afterwards as a member of educational policy commissions, exhorting schools to strengthen their academic offerings and calling attention to unconscionable variances between support for schools in slums and suburbs. In the 1980s, Donald Kennedy, president of Stanford University, convened a university study panel on "the university and the schools" and encouraged faculty to visit and do research on California schools and to participate in projects that would reform and improve the schools. Boston University President Silber's proposal was still bolder in asserting that his university could actually manage the schools of a city such as Boston or Chelsea and achieve more satisfactory results.

What can universities do to help schools? First, universities collect superior intellects in every field of knowledge. Second, universities have many persons skilled in setting goals, in designing evaluation systems, in writing curriculums, and in generating proposals for raising money. These talents are needed by public school systems. Also, some university professors know how to challenge the status quo and puncture complacency and substandard performance. Although submitting to a critique is not always pleasant, many city schools require this scrutiny and a challenge to seek excellence.

2. City schools need the same quality and quantity of citizen involvement as do the suburbs or rural areas. During the 1980s, big city schools had very little parent or community input, especially at the school level, and the central bureaucracies running the schools too often seemed to stultify initiatives at the school-site level.

While the early wave of reform in the 1980s called for increased state goal setting, testing, and inspection, the school reform tide after 1985 turned toward stimulating individual school principals, teachers, and parents to assume greater responsibilities. Many small suburban school systems and the most successful private schools excel in part because of the intense focus on the individual school, the students, and their needs. Opinions differ on whether the teachers or the parents should have the majority of seats on a local school council, on whether the principal should be the chair of the council, and on whether the rest of the neighborhood or political community should have seats at the table. These issues are eclipsed by matters of scope. For example, should the selection of textbooks and materials be done by a central authority or by the individual school? Should the principal be assigned, selected, retained, or fired by the local school council?

How much leeway should be given? How much authority over the program should be given to the local school?

Chicago pursues a very aggressive version of the old New England school committee mode—a Puritan model of "every tub on its own bottom." The advantages lean in the direction of allowing parent control over the mission of the school, discretion over how to use resources, and relative speed in getting rid of unimaginative leadership. Many schools could be energized and stimulated to improve if this plan works in the city.

3. Reform itself requires new sources of support and energy. Schools in many cities have lost much of the once strong parental political constituencies. In too many communities, public school parents account for only 10 percent of the voters. Parents of school-age children by themselves can no longer pass a school bond issue or set a new tax levy. There must be an alliance, a coalition of community persons and colleges and employers. Schools can neither gather enough resources by themselves nor reform the schools nor upgrade performance without outside help. Schools exist not only to serve students but to assist the larger society in achieving certain expectations about the quality of life, the work force, and the community. When schools fail to meet those expectations, one remedy is to let other citizens into the decision-making process.

As strong as those arguments may be, other points of view on school reform must be considered. Among the more cautious perspectives are the following:

1. Universities should concentrate on core functions such as scholarship, research, and teaching and not try to run complicated institutions for the rest of society. Colleges and universities serve a selective clientele and may lack the competence needed to help the rest of a community. There are exceptions. Many of the great research universities run teaching hospitals. Some of them are located in low-income neighborhoods and reach out to the most disadvantaged patients. One private university, the University of Chicago, operates its Laboratory School with approximately fifteen hundred students. Elsewhere in the nation, however, the campus laboratory schools too often become conservative in pedagogy, cautious in seeking clientele other than children of college faculty, perform more like an anchor rather than a catalyst in school reform elsewhere, and certainly do not meet nonuniversity community needs.

Universities tend to be impatient with the problems of little children and the lower schools. Again there are exceptions. Seymour Papert, of the Massachusetts Institute of Technology, worked with a Boston elementary school exploring computer possibilities. James Comer of Yale University helps the schools in New Haven. Theodore Sizer of Brown University formed the Coalition of Essential Schools. Of course, not all university prescriptions will cure what ails the public schools. Previous assistance in the form of the "new mathematics" or new science curricula came out of great universities but did not prevent reduced enthusiasm for mathematics and science courses in American schools.

Finally, there is the issue of management. President John Silber's decision to have Boston University run a school system was extraordinary. But even if Boston University enjoys great success, it may be difficult to find other university presidents willing to shoulder responsibility for a low-achieving school system. The arguments or explanations will be plausible: "The role of the university is to criticize other entities in society, not to take them over." Or, "We have too many problems, too many unmet financial needs of our own." Or, "Our university cannot run a school system; we have difficulty keeping our own campus healthy and safe and our faculty satisfied."

Peter Goldmark, president of the Rockefeller Foundation, studied the Boston University–Chelsea proposal and questioned the replicability of the model. If Chelsea needed $1 million, would New York City because of its size require $200 million to make the same model work?

In summary, there may be a very limited university taste for assuming full responsibility for a school system. And there are many more school systems in trouble than there are great-hearted universities. However, Boston University may demonstrate the usefulness of urban education reform strategies that can be implemented with or without university involvement.

2. The rural-suburban model of local control or site management may not be the ideal model for city school governance in the 1990s or for the twenty-first century. Some families and their children will not stay in a city neighborhood for more than a year or two and that is why a citywide curriculum is so desirable. Many neighborhoods, especially in Chicago, are all black or all Hispanic. Additional ways must be found to overcome decades of racial isolation, separation, and segregation. After the initial euphoria about school councils, the local school may become vulnerable to local neighborhood contests over

jobs, contracts, and political power. The school may need some insulation from corrupting elements in the neighborhood.

3. The remedy for the improvement of urban schools may be none of the above. Support grows nationally for developing a new coalition of schools, health workers, and social service providers. The schools cannot alone overcome malnutrition, physical and emotional disabilities, unstable family and home environments, drug- and crime-infested environments, and other maladies. The concept of the school as a free-standing organization independent of general-purpose government needs intensive scrutiny. One proposal is for cities to have a Youth Services Cabinet (health, social service, police, employment, education) with assignments closely coordinated.

Education in cities may also need to rely much more heavily on instructional technology. The chalkboard and jawbone sufficient for the early twentieth century will not suffice as the efficient tools for learning that will be required in the twenty-first century. Videodiscs, integrated learning systems, and computer software will become essential components of instruction at school, at home, and at the workplace. Education has generally resisted technology, but the number 2 pencil and the pad of paper will eventually give way to sophisticated communications and learning systems. Whatever governance system is adopted should abet and accelerate the wise use of technology. This is easy to say but will be difficult to implement if school councils with less than adequate competence could veto promising technological proposals.

Who should make decisions about the use of technology in education? A national panel? A state board or council? Given the atomized, fragmented nature of education in the United States, it could happen that well-to-do suburbs will capture the lead and a decade later the lowest-income children in the inner city may hopefully gain access to the latest instructional technology.

These reservations should not be ignored by policymakers or by proponents of urban education reform. Nor can an unwilling university be mandated to adopt an ailing, failing school system. Nor can the United States believe that extreme local control of schools is the full answer to survival or competitive success against industrial nations with centrally funded and coordinated educational systems. Each child needs strong support from the family and strong financial resources from the state if educational goals and societal expectations are to be fulfilled.

ASSESSING THE NEW MODELS FOR SCHOOL GOVERNANCE

Have Chicago and Chelsea found the keys to school improvement? How soon can other cities borrow from, adopt, or adapt their solutions?

Even the most active proponents ask for enough time to prove the worth of the urban experiments. Boston University's John Silber and Chicago's Donald Moore insist that as much as ten years may be needed to demonstrate genuine effectiveness. This will not satisfy impatient journalists and others who want spectacular short-term results. Moreover, there is the issue of the appropriateness of the intervention. Is it enough to harness the resources of a great university? Will it suffice to make principals more accountable for progress to a council of parents, teachers, and community representatives? Furthermore, no single strategy, however effective, will be sufficient. For example, preschool assistance for nutrition and for pre- and postnatal care will be exceptionally important for children in the inner city. But such interventions at early childhood, important as they are for improving life chances of inner-city children who are at risk, will need to be sustained through their later years as well.

It will be surprising if changing the governance structure alone solves the problems of urban education. The governance system provides both a process for change and a forum for argument about such important matters as resource allocation. In the 1990s, hardly anyone felt that the top-down, centralist, look-alike school configuration would provide the cure for stagnation in urban schools. The test will be whether the new models of governance will advance the opportunity for increased educational productivity or whether they will create new distractions, diversions, and distortions, as in the late-nineteenth-century complaints about decentralized urban governance.

By 1990, New York State Commissioner of Education Thomas Sobol called for the abolition of New York City's central school board and the creation of autonomous school districts within the city. Similar proposals were made to the Illinois legislature in the 1970s. These proposals clearly would reduce the scale of decision making regarding urban schools. They would, however, lock in the provincialism of boroughs and wards and neighborhoods. Whether they will lead to the promotion of good citizenship, racial harmony, and student achievement remains a very open question.

Will city school boards be needed at all in the twenty-first century? In 1939, a commentator on issues in public administration called the urban school board "one of those instruments of tortuous propensities which, beaming with unbecoming and reflected wisdom, wanders in a twilight zone between civil squander and political connivance. Undoubtedly, some future public appraisal, beyond the board's discernment, will snuff it out" (Hodges, 1939, pp. 680–681). In Chelsea, the question is raised as to whether the local school board is really needed if the Boston University team accomplishes most of its objectives. Perhaps a corporate model, an urban board meeting once each quarter, will emerge as a compromise nod to citizen control of urban schools.

Corporate or civic reformers cannot place their bets on reform in school governance alone. The history of urban school board reform indicates that this strategy never worked in the last century. As T. S. Eliot suggests, "It is not possible to design governments so perfect that men no longer need to be good." The education of city children must ever be a central priority for business and labor, for foundations and universities, for general government officials—indeed for all who have a concern for the future of urban education.

REFERENCES

Boston University. *Boston University Plan for Chelsea Public Schools.* Boston: Boston University, 1988.

Charter Revision Commission for New York City. *The Impact of School Decentralization in New York City on Municipal Decentralization.* New York: Charter Revision Commission for New York City, June 1974.

Chelsea Oversight Panel. *Report on the First Year of Implementation of the Chelsea School Committee-Boston University Agreement, 1989–1990.* Boston: Boston University, November 1990.

Chicago United. *The Chicago School System.* Report of the Special Task Force on Education. Chicago: Chicago United, 1981.

Chicago United. *Agenda for Public Education in Chicago.* Chicago: Chicago United, 1983.

Chicago United. *Reassessment of the Report of the 1981 Special Task Force on Education.* Chicago: Chicago United, 1987.

Chicago United and Roosevelt University, Center for American Policy Studies. *Education for a New Illinois: The Public Schools in a Changing Economy.* Chicago: Chicago United and Roosevelt University, 1985.

Cronin, Joseph M. *The Control of Urban Schools.* New York: Free Press, 1973.

Cronin, Joseph M. *Big City School Bankruptcy*. Stanford, Calif. Stanford Institute for Finance and Governance, Stanford University, 1981.

Designs for Change. "Progress in Year One." In *Closer Look*, No. 1. Chicago: Designs for Change, February 1991.

Gittell, Marilyn. "School Governance." In *Setting Municipal Priorities*, edited by Charles Brecher and Raymond D. Horton. Montclair, N.J.: Allan, Held, Osman, 1980.

Greer, Peter. *The Boston University-Chelsea Public Schools First Annual Report, September 1989–June 30, 1990*. Boston: Boston University, 1990.

Hill, Paul P.; Wise, Arthur E.; and Shapiro, Leslie. *Educational Progress: Cities Mobilize to Improve Their Schools*. New York: Rand Corporation, 1989.

Hodges, Harry. *City Management*. New York: F. S. Crofts, 1939.

Institute for Responsive Education. *Tuning in to Chelsea Public School Parents: A Survey*. Boston: Institute for Responsive Education, 1990.

Kirst, Michael. "Central Office Confusion Perils School Reform," *Catalyst* 2, no. 3 (1990): 15–19.

Manasian, David. "Success and Excess: A Survey of California," *Economist* 317 (October 13, 1990): 1–22.

Mayor's Advisory Panel on Decentralization of the New York City Schools. *Recommendation for Learning: A Community School System for New York City*. New York: Mayor's Advisory Panel on Decentralization of the New York City Schools, 1967.

Mitchner, Mary Francis. "The Long Haul: The Chicago Business Community/Chicago Public School Reform." Unpublished paper. Cambridge, Mass.: Kennedy School of Government, Harvard University, 1989.

Moore, Donald. *Voice and Choice in Chicago*. Chicago: Designs for Change, 1989.

Moore, Donald. *Some Facts about the First Year of Chicago School Reform*. Chicago: Designs for Change, 1990.

National School Boards Association, *School Board News*, 14 August 1990, p. 4.

Newsweek. "Not a Miracle Cure," *Newsweek*, 17 September 1990.

Poinsett, Alex. "Chicago Reform Activists Say 'No' to School Choice," *Catalyst* 2, no. 3 (1990): 3.

Shanker, Albert. Quoted in *Bostonia*, November-December, 1989. Pp. 35–37.

Shannon, Thomas A. "Chelsea's Peril Is Poverty, Not B.U." *American School Board Journal* 176, no. 6 (June 1989): 49.

Viteritti, Joseph P. *Across the River: Politics and Education in the City*. New York: Holmer and Meier, 1983.

Walberg, Herbert J., and Bakalis, Michael. *We Can Rescue Our Children*. Ottawa, Canada: Greenhill Publishers, 1988.

Washington Monthly. "The Joker Who Runs Our Schools," September 1990, p. 12.

CHAPTER 5

State Takeovers and Other Last Resorts

Sally Bulkley Pancrazio

Public attention was captured when the State of New Jersey used its powers to assume the administrative responsibility for the Jersey City school system. Although state takeovers have had a long history in American education and other school districts have been threatened with state takeover, Jersey City, in 1989, was the first school district recently to have been actually taken over. Nine states have takeover statutes: Arkansas, Georgia, Kentucky, New Jersey, New Mexico, Ohio, South Carolina, Texas, and West Virginia (Pipho, 1991). More state legislatures will consider the efficacy of similar statutes as the debate about the quality of American schools

The author wishes to acknowledge particularly the work and words of Elena Scambio, State District Superintendent, Jersey City School System; Saul Cooperman, former Commissioner of Education, New Jersey Department of Education; Betty E. Steffy, Deputy Superintendent of Instruction, Kentucky Department of Education, and last, but never least, Nelson F. Ashline, former Executive Deputy Superintendent, Illinois Department of Education, in the preparation of this chapter. Any errors of interpretation of their insights and observations are, of course, the author's own.

continues. It is a reflection of the times, with diminishing public confidence in the schools, that states are now more aggressively seeking such power (as in, e.g., Kentucky and West Virginia) and using it (as in New Jersey).

Although the term *state takeover* was first used to describe actions taken by a state department of education to monitor fiscal soundness and financial practices in its school districts, the term has only recently been applied in some states to issues of academic performance in schools and school districts. This is no accident. The earliest information provided to state departments of education included numbers of students, where they were enrolled, and how much money was being spent to educate them. One wag said: "If institutions were known by the information collected about them, school districts would be banks." Fiscal management took precedence over academic performance.

During the 1980s, however, the public disquiet with the results of various measures of student performance, such as achievement test scores, forced issues of education and schooling to the national, state, and local forefront. While educators asked legislators and governors for more money to do their jobs more effectively, state legislatures asked educators for greater accountability as the resources were being expended. This accountability began to mean that the public had a right to expect a fair return for the money it invested in education. Today, the issues of cost and performance are inexorably linked in matters of public policy.

This chapter answers the following questions regarding state takeovers of public schools: What is a takeover? What is a state's authority to assume a takeover of schools? What is the role of a state education agency? What is the argument for a state takeover? What conditions describe a school district ripe for state takeover? What evidence exists that state takeovers work?

WHAT IS A STATE TAKEOVER?

A state takeover refers to an action taken by a state department of education, approved by the state board of education and authorized by statute, to assume administrative responsibility for a given public school district for a specified period of time. This action is taken by the state when it determines, through a deliberate review and a progressively intrusive process, that the school district cannot or will not meet prescribed standards. The chief state school officer (the state commissioner or state superintendent) removes the district superintendent and appoints a new administrator who in turn may replace other key school officials, particularly business-finance, curriculum, or personnel positions, and building principals. An advisory board from the local community may be appointed by the chief to replace the sitting local school board.

Generally, a state takeover occurs when state officials determine that actions required by the state and taken by the local school district to correct deficiencies have not brought the improvement required by state standards. While a district may have existed for years with dire enough conditions to warrant takeover, two conditions have to be present for a state to initiate takeover: the existence of statutory power and the appropriate social and political climate to exercise that power. Often just the threat of a takeover succeeds in bringing about the conditions necessary for compliance and improvement. A state takeover is meant as a last resort to improve the conditions of schooling.

Because the right to take over schools and districts is founded in state law, there are plenty of opportunities for school officials to shape the conditions of the initial legislation, to use the pressure of the threat to persuade the community to assist in the improvement process (such as a passage of a needed bond and tax referendum), and to use the power of the judicial process at any step of the review. In other words, the local school board and the district administrators retain considerable power and decision making up to the point when a state board of education or court decides in favor of the legitimacy of the state takeover. When the school district meets the established standards, the school district is returned to local control with a new school board and new superintendent.

The term *state takeover* may in fact be a misnomer. The term implies that the state assumes total control of the local school or district and makes decisions without any knowledge of local conditions or input from local sources. This is not true. A takeover cannot occur independently from the legislative, executive, and judicial processes (which, granted, are state entities). Community representatives appointed to serve on an interim board in an advisory capacity provide local flavor to the school debates. As Henry Marks (1991), staff person in the Kentucky State Department of Education, said, "The difficulty in takeover lies in the word itself."

State takeover does not mean the abandonment of local personnel or local advice. State takeover does mean that the state temporarily assumes policymaking and administrative leadership for the district. Other terms associated with the sanction of takeover include state receivership, trusteeship, academic bankruptcy, and academic deficiency, although the last two terms describe a condition of the district that led to the sanction, not the sanction itself.

WHAT IS A STATE'S AUTHORITY TO TAKE OVER SCHOOLS?

In the United States, by delegation in our federal Constitution and by designation in each state constitution, the education of all persons within a state and the quality of that education is a primary function of state government, regardless of the amount of financing provided by local governments. The state has a compelling interest to educate its citizens to the fullest extent possible, so that the affairs of government can continue to be conducted in a way that is responsive to the needs of its citizens and their present and future quality of life. In practice, the responsibility for addressing the educational needs and interests of the state lies in a two-tiered system of state and local government. As Thomas Guskey (1990) said:

> From a legal perspective, state officials have both the right and responsibility to operate institutions of public education. Although historically states have opted to share this responsibility with local school officials, it remains clear that decisions regarding control rest with the state.

In education, the agency that has the designated state responsibility is, of course, the state department of education, whose administration is led by a chief state school officer and whose policies are set by an appointed or elected state board of education (except in Wisconsin). As part of the political process, the state legislature and governor, lobbyists, and all interested parties give their opinions and exercise their responsibilities to influence the direction and strength of state action. The system can be agonizingly slow, unwieldily resistant, or shallow, but it is the checks and balances of the system that preserves our democratic society.

By statute, regulation, or advisory guidelines, the state sets benchmarks, expectations, or minimum standards that schools or school districts must meet. Schools must meet such minimum standards to operate without state intervention (including technical assistance) or sanctions. Our system of government is such that the people (parents, community activists, professionals, policymakers at all levels) exercise their right to express their views of the character and nature of the statute, regulation, or guideline.

WHAT IS THE ROLE OF THE STATE EDUCATION AGENCY?

The state has two roles in education: regulatory and excellence. The major distinction between these two roles is in the state's impact on local schools, communities, and students. The regulatory role is compulsory. The excellence role is voluntary. A principle of voluntary action on the part of the school and its board and officials is inherent in its establishing standards of quality. The state will *not* prevent a school district from being the best it can be. However, the state does have an obligation as part of its public trust to take reasonable action to assure that the schools meet certain minimum requirements.

The primary mission of all state departments of education, most often led by their state board of education, includes regulating the schools; providing leadership and guidance to schools; distributing the state and federal monies to school districts; collecting, analyzing, and reporting information useful to determine the relative condition of education within the state; and setting educational policy. State departments of education take a full range of actions to conduct their business.

The actions of the state department of education follow a continuum of less prescriptive to more prescriptive. These include technical assistance, in which resources are provided to local schools, often on request; exhortation and encouragement through incentives and setting of examples; and state monitoring to assure that minimum standards are met.

Sanctions—generically referred to as state interventions—may include, depending on state statutes and regulations, withholding specific state funds, state takeovers, state receiverships, school consolidations, and the ultimate action, school closings and the dissolution of the school district. Sanctions are clearly last resorts, not first recourses.

Further, the local school district, through the appeal and judicial procedures open to its local board of education, reserves the right to dispute the state's case and go to court over the matter. In Kentucky, two county school systems were threatened with state takeover because of noncompliance with academic standards. The Whitley County school system went to court, sued, and won. By extension, then, no further action was taken in the Floyd County school system. Therefore, even under the cloud of possible state takeovers, a local school system maintains some control over its destiny.

None of the sanctions a state department of education can take can occur without the approval of the state's general assembly and governor. The authority for the sanctions emerges from statute. And, like all political processes, sanctions are open to the scrutiny of the public. If the elected representatives of the people do not want the state department to have the authority to make specific interventions into the affairs of a particular school, the process will not allow the state department either to begin or to conclude that intervention.

The extent to which a state department of education in fact aggressively uses its legal and constitutional authority and responsibility depends, of course, on the strength of the leadership of the state board and the chief state school officer, and their sense of the political and social climate.

WHAT IS THE ARGUMENT FOR A STATE TAKEOVER?

Four dimensions undergird the argument for a state takeover: the emergence of learner outcomes and other academic standards to measure the quality of schooling; the use of information indicators as proxies for those measures; the need for children's interests to be paramount in school decisions; and the belief that schools matter.

The Presence of Learner Outcomes and Other Academic Standards

First, in establishing goals for educational outcomes, the state designates (with considerable advice from the public) what it believes are important academic expectations for learners as a consequence of their having attended the schools in that state. These outcomes can be explicit or implicit.

States communicate their expectations for learning in state-developed tests that directly assess what the states want students to learn, or they assess learning through the use of commonly accepted national tests. The results of these tests may have implications for students' promotion or graduation. While virtually all states now have testing systems to assess student performance, Ramsay Seldon, Director of the State Education Assessment Center of the Council of Chief State School Officers, says that in many states, achievement goals now provide the framework for state assessment of curriculum in at least reading and mathematics.

As an example of explicit statement of outcomes, the 1985 Illinois Educational Reform Act contained 169 provisions. The capstone of the act included a definition of the primary purpose of schooling and a provision giving the state board of education the authority to identify state learning goals. It did so; learning goals were established in six areas: language arts, mathematics, reading, science, physical health and development, and fine arts. Its state assessment tests (or will test) in these six areas. Other states have similar expectations for learning and assessment mechanisms.

In summary, state departments of education are moving toward identifying academic outcomes and then holding school districts accountable for achieving those outcomes.

Information Indicators

Second, the public's need and desire to evaluate the cost of public services commensurate with the public funds to support those services is way ahead of the profession's knowledge of how to measure the worth of the services. Because these services—schools, health, safety, transportation—cost so much in relation to a family's capacity to support itself, we are only now, relatively speaking, asking how we will know whether some service is worth what we spend on it. Because we cannot measure worth directly (e.g., how do we know students are really learning?), we look at indicators of the thing we value.

An indicator is a statistic attached to something we value, often expressed as a percentage such as the percentage of students graduating or the percentage of students going on to college. As an indicator of student achievement, the state's learning outcomes are often measured by the scores from state testing or assessment systems. Or, scores from nationally normed tests, such as the SAT (Scholastic Aptitude Test) or tests of the American College Testing Program (ACT), are used to show how well a given group of students in a school is doing. While student learning is clearly the primary reason why schools exist, the many criticisms of standardized test scores preclude their being the sole measure of the effectiveness of the school and the schooling process. Test scores are, however, the most common measure of the quality of schooling that the public wants to see. Until there are better measures of school effectiveness, test scores, with all their flaws, are the bottom line for schooling. Other commonly used indicators to assess the effectiveness of schooling include promotion and graduation.

Since schools are complex social systems that attempt both to transmit the culture (inculcation of cultural values) and to influence the culture (improve and reform our culture), the conditions under which schools operate are connected with how well they achieve their mission. Children's learning is affected by the resources available for schooling, the distribution of those resources, and the capacity of the school to make a difference in children's learning. As a result, the need for information about schooling, including achievement, becomes paramount.

The profession is becoming more sophisticated in framing what information it needs to make judgments, particularly in the extremes, such as the highly desirable or the most unsatisfactory. In both New Jersey and Kentucky, a curriculum audit was used to evaluate how well a school was performing (English, 1990). State departments of education use such terms as *comprehensive curriculum audits* or *audit probes* to describe the basis for their school reviews. The new Kentucky Educational Reform Act calls for a performance assessment coupled with a student achievement baseline established for each school (Steffy, 1990b). To certify its schools, New Jersey monitors ten key areas: curriculum and instruction, staff, student attendance, basic skills, mandated programs (such as special education), planning and financial management, facilities, the relationship with the community, and policies regarding equal educational opportunity (Cooperman, 1989).

A recent report to the Illinois State Board of Education from an advisory group charged with examining the state's current procedures for regulating public schools and for strengthening accountability in Illinois schools urged the use of state standards, including state test scores and rates for attendance, graduation, dropping out, and expulsion, as indicators of performance (Banas, 1991). Schools failing to meet standards would be required to establish school-based improvement goals. While Illinois school districts have been required since 1986 to release information on the performance of their four thousand schools and 1.8 million students, the information is not yet linked to any state action. Further, the recommendations call for examining the "the school's parent involvement, curriculum, teaching, environment and leadership in helping it to determine how to correct shortcomings" (Banas, 1991).

The categories of state intervention include "technical assistance, academic watch list, administrative oversight, and imposed change of a school's operations" (Illinois State Board of Education, 1991). Sanctions such as school mergers, closing schools, and firing the superintendent were identified, as well as various rewards or incentives for improved school performance. Members of the public, not bureaucrats, argued for state sanctions.

State departments of education, and the people who advise them, are accepting the use of indicators of school performance, including test scores, as a basis for judging how well schools are doing. As states become more sophisticated in framing and displaying these indicators and in analyzing the information, the indicators will likely become the bases for state action such as incentives and sanctions including takeovers. The state department of education intervenes in local schools because it must and no other entity has the capacity to do so.

The Children's Interests

Third, state takeovers recognize the political arena in which education plays and the unique position of quarterback played by state boards and chief state school officers. When all other key players act in defense of special interest groups and constituencies, someone must call the plays on behalf of the children.

Illustrating this view in New Jersey, former Commissioner of Education Saul Cooperman (1988) said of state takeovers, "It's a step we will take reluctantly—as a last resort—when it is the only way we can guarantee students their right to a good education." Similarly, Betty E. Steffy (1990a), Deputy Superintendent in the Kentucky Department of Education said, "If a state agency is not willing to confront ineffective districts and demand improvement, who will? If a state agency decides not to intervene, the children attending schools in these ineffective districts are doomed indefinitely to a substandard education."

Cooperman (1989) emphasizes the link between the state's interest in an educated citizenry and the future of the state's welfare itself when he says, "We cannot allow a few irresponsible local boards to deny their students opportunities the students will need for their futures. If we fail these children, we fail ourselves."

While specific members of a state board are not immune to the influence of special interests, it is the responsibility of the state board members as a group to work to transcend local, partisan, and specific special interests for the good of the children of the state. Parents cannot automatically do this, as they must necessarily speak to the interests of their individual children, and not to those of children as a whole. Legislators and governors must balance the state's resources among agencies in competition with education, such as health, transportation, public safety, and economic development. State school boards cannot afford the parochialism of some local boards whose interests end where local school boundaries end.

Schools Matter

Last, an inherent belief that schools, and those who lead them, influence children's lives provides the moral thrust and educational rationale for state interventions such as takeovers. Although the results of the effective schools literature will not be reviewed here, a main message from that literature is pertinent: "Some schools obtain much better student achievement than others that have similar resources and serve similar populations" (Guskey, 1990).

Yet, the message seems not to have gotten across to all school administrators. A sense of helplessness and a loss of control too often pervades their conversations, and thereby their actions. One superintendent testified at a public meeting that "children in my district are dumber than children in (richer) districts." Another said, "We know the IQs of kids at _____ School are low. These kids can't learn any more even though I have my best teachers there." From a third, "I wish parents would take better care of their kids. They come to school unfed, unlearned, and unloved and we can't do anything with them."

When Jersey City was threatened initially with state takeover, its superintendent was quoted in *Newsweek* as saying (Leslie, Emerson, and Wingert, 1989, p. 63), "Jersey City's problem is not incompetence. It's money and a poor population." To school board members, the same superintendent is quoted as saying, "Show me an urban school system that does not have serious problems" (Reecer, 1988).

Granted, there are immense challenges for providing good schooling in schools with a majority of poor children, but not all urban districts in New Jersey were cited for not meeting minimum state standards over consecutive periods of time. In fairness, one has to contrast these examples of helplessness and blaming the children for the inadequacy of the school experience with superintendents well grounded in educational research and practice and a belief that the school system can indeed make a difference.

In describing how his particular school system assures stability in instruction for highly mobile children, an Illinois urban superintendent said, "We send a bus for the kids, no matter where they moved to, and we bring them back to their home school," thus assuring these children of a stable and continuing instructional environment.

Or there is the principal whose school, located in a public housing project in Chicago, was plagued by parental indifference. She got parents to come to her school in the evening by first going to their churches to talk to them. Her teachers then collected their old but still usable children's clothes and sold them for $1 a paper sack full, with the money going to the school. Parents came out. Another time, the principal persuaded the local food pantry to donate cartons of tuna fish, and the cafeteria cooks volunteered to prepare a tuna casserole dinner for the whole family before parent-teacher conferences. More parents came to school.

Once parents viewed the school as friendly turf, communication between teachers and parents focused on what they could do collectively to support their children's learning. "We'll do whatever we have to do," the principal said. "We know schools matter."

According to John Duncan (1988), in a presentation to the California School Boards Association, the California Superintendents Association identified a series of belief statements prepared in response to the potential of the use of state takeovers of "at risk schools where a cycle of failure was found to be present." The statements recognize realistically that "schools alone cannot resolve or be accountable for all social, economic, and environmental obstacles which students face," but they also underscore the relevance of high expectations for students and school accountability.

The first statement says, "Superintendents and administrators should be held accountable for the management of the schools with other staff sharing accountability for the quality of instruction provided to students." School accountability begins with its leaders. It is no accident that in a school district takeover by the state, the board and its superintendent are the first to be removed.

The second statement says, "All students can learn when schools provide a positive learning environment with dedicated and committed administrators, teachers, and support staff." The belief that schools matter is explicit.

Among the beliefs held by the Regulatory Process Committee, the advisory committee that recommends improvements in the regulation of Illinois schools, are the following: schools should be places where "all children can learn," where "all children must be served," and where "high expectations are necessary to achieve a world-class education" (Illinois State Board of Education, 1991). Beliefs that schools matter increase the likelihood that school improvement happens and children learn.

WHAT CONDITIONS DESCRIBE A SCHOOL DISTRICT OR SCHOOL RIPE FOR STATE TAKEOVER?

Some conditions that describe a school district or school ripe for takeover, assuming that the state has passed legislation giving it authority to exercise takeover power, are discussed in the following paragraphs.

The school district exhibits failure year after year. A prime candidate for takeover has a record of not meeting state minimum standards for several consecutive years, particularly in the areas of finance, building safety, and academic standards. Other state actions have yielded no significant changes in the record of the school district.

The school district is plagued by patronage, nepotism, and corruption. Hiring practices are based on personal relationships. There is evidence of influence peddling. Nepotism, favoritism, and political sponsorship are rampant when contracts are let and personnel hired. Staff are demoralized and express their feelings of loss of professional control over their lives. The school district may be the largest employer in the community, and hence, decisions are based on economics and power rather than on children's interest and schooling considerations.

The school district has a history of noncooperation with the state department of education. A state department as an agency prefers to work out disagreements with school districts rather than going to the mat. A sanction like a state takeover becomes a distinct possibility when the school district is unable or unwilling (terms used in both New Jersey and Kentucky) to solve its own problems or work cooperatively with the state department of education, using the technical assistance provided by the state to solve the problems.

Forces outside the school district call for its reform. There has to be a political and social structure to support the state department of education as it pursues a state takeover of a school district. When the situation gets to the point where a local school or district cannot improve (because of lack of ability to support improvement) or will not (due either to the educational management or to intransigence by the school board), other forces stimulate or reinforce the state's intervention. Parent groups, business, community activists, opinion makers, and legislators provide that reinforcement.

WHAT EVIDENCE EXISTS THAT STATE TAKEOVERS WORK?

The potential for state takeover can generate reform. The threat of the state department of education taking any of these sanctions may produce the desired effect. For example, Saul Cooperman (1989) reports that of the sixteen school districts in New Jersey that did not receive state certification (certified as meeting the state's minimum standards in ten areas), the Jersey City school system was the only district taken over by the state. Other school districts identified as substandard at that time obtained the will and the way to take corrective action sufficient to bring their schools into compliance.

Is state takeover working in Jersey City? "The jury is still out, but we are doing everything possible to make it work," says Jeffrey Graber

(1991), executive assistant to Elena Scambio, the school superintendent appointed to the Jersey City school system by the New Jersey
Commissioner of Education.

After the New Jersey State Board of Education approved the
takeover in Jersey City, the local school board sued the state board to
halt state intervention, and the matter went to court. In August 1989,
the administrative law judge upheld the opinion that the state should
take over the Jersey City system. The state department of education
assumed control in October 1989.

Dr. Graber (1991) says the "situation was a disaster. Teachers and
principals who were assigned to the central office and were paid
salaries of $50,000 to $60,000 either didn't show up for work or had no
defined roles." Building principals had not been evaluated in any
orderly, systematic manner for some time. Classrooms had remained
unpainted for thirty years. Students scored at the bottom on state
tests. Even after four years of in-depth study of the school system, the
state-appointed staff, upon assuming control, found problems shock-
ing. The local school board was dissolved, and an advisory board of
education was established with thirteen members appointed by the
New Jersey Commissioner of Education and two members from the
local municipality.

The interim board is composed of men and women whose ethnicity,
professions, and backgrounds are representative of their community.
By selecting local people to guide the reconstruction of the dysfunctional school district, the state dissolved the influence of the bad-apple
leadership and in effect established the means to return the district to
local control with a powerful new beginning.

By April 1990, School Superintendent Scambio had implemented a
central office reorganization wherein all positions in the central office
were abolished. After an assessment of personnel and of the needs of
the new organization, people were returned to their positions, demoted, or their employment was terminated. Rules established
through tenure and civil service were followed as required by the
takeover legislation. Dr. Scambio hired thirty-eight staff, a balance
between insiders and outsiders, to bring new ideas to the district. In
all, 117 persons in this district of thirty thousand children were
terminated, reassigned, or demoted.

State technical assistance followed the state takeover. Some monies
were provided through the Quality Education Assistance Act to help
the thirty urban school systems in New Jersey. A comprehensive
personnel assessment was undertaken, with assistance from state

department of education staff and an independent consulting firm. Questions are being raised about the nearly $8 million spent on medical benefits for 250 employees no longer working in the district. Three of these individuals were deceased.

Superintendent Scambio's motto is "Kids First." She said, "This was a district where jobs, money, and power were the prime motivators. We had to change the mindset. It was a humongous task to institute a new focus on kids" (Scambio, 1991). From the school custodians to the senior managers in the school system, every person is being held accountable for his or her performance. "We came into a school system where no one wanted us, except the parents," she said. A specific effort is being undertaken to involve the parents of the children of Jersey City in the reform activities and this effort will extend the mantle of accountability.

Dr. Graber (1991) emphasized that "it would be wrong to assume that all the teachers and administrators in the Jersey City schools were performing poorly. There are some very fine people in the district. They just had not been given the opportunity to excel or get the job done." Now, there is a new life to the school system and a better hope for the future of thirty thousand children.

By law, Dr. Scambio must report on the status of the Jersey City schools to the state board of education and the New Jersey legislature. How will she measure success? Her response: "We'll look at the reduction in dropout rates, increased student and staff attendance, and over time, increased student achievement" (Scambio 1991). After experiencing a declining enrollment over the years, similar to most other urban school systems, Jersey City had an increase of eight hundred students who transferred in from nonpublic schools, which is clearly a signal of public confidence.

CONCLUSION

The trend across the states is for more severe state intervention in low-performing school districts, while at the same time reformers are calling for greater flexibility and decision making at the local level. Thomas Shannon (in Leslie, Emerson, and Wingert, 1989), speaking for the National Association of School Boards, said, "They (the state) should give us more tools and less rules." Chris Pipho (1991) refers to these trends as "countervailing," because there are examples of momentous moves in large districts like Chicago and New York to shift decision making from the centralized boards to the local schools.

In fact, however, these two trends are not in opposition. They are part of the state legislatures and state departments of education coming to recognize the state can and must specify what students need to know and be able to do as a result of their schooling while at the same time permitting local schools to better determine how to assure that students and schools meet these expectations. The state determines the outcomes, the local system determines how it will best reach those outcomes, and the state monitors the outcomes. The trends are harmonious, not dissonant.

When local boards fail, and their appointed school leaders fail, there has to be a means by which a radical intervention can be made in a dysfunctional school system. Used sparingly and fairly, state takeovers offer an essential last resort to improve America's schools.

REFERENCES

Banas, Casey. "New State Standards Urged for Schools," *Chicago Tribune*, 21 February 1991, pp. 1, 8.

Cooperman, Saul. "'We Prefer to Motivate Deficient Schools, but—If Pushed—We'll Regulate Them, Too,'" *American School Board Journal* 175 (November 1988): 24–25.

Cooperman, Saul. "Intervention in Deficient School Districts: Reestablishing Effective Local Control." Paper presented at the convention of the American Association of School Administrators, Orlando, Flor., March 1989.

Duncan, John W. "Academic Accountability and State Intervention." Paper presented at the annual conference of the California School Boards Association, Los Angeles, Calif., December 1988.

English, Fenwick. "Creating Prescriptions for State Takeovers of Local School Districts: A Reflective Critique." Paper presented at the annual meeting of the American Educational Research Association, Boston, 1990.

Graber, Jeffrey, Personal conversation, March 26, 1991.

Guskey, Thomas R. "Policy Issues and Options When States Take Over Local School Districts." Paper presented at the annual meeting of the American Educational Research Association, Boston, 1990.

Illinois State Board of Education. *News*, 20 February 1991, pp. 1–5.

Leslie, Connie; Emerson, Tony; and Wingert, Pat. "Very Hostile Takeovers: States May Step in When Local Schools Fail," *Newsweek*, 13 March 1989, p. 63.

Marks, Henry. Personal conversation, March 3, 1991.

Pipho, Chris. Personal conversation, 1991.

Reecer, Marcia. "Jersey City Stands Firm against Charges of 'Academic Bankruptcy.'" *American School Board Journal* 175 (November 1988): 21–23.

Scambio, Elena. Personal conversation, March 5, 1991.

Steffy, Betty E. "Dilemmas Presented by State Agency Takeovers of Local School Districts." Paper presented at the annual meeting of the American Educational Research Association, Boston, 1990a.

Steffy, Betty E. "Can Rational Organizational Models Really Reform Anything? A Case Study of Kentucky Reform." Paper presented at the meeting of the University Council of Educational Administration, Pittsburgh, 1990b.

Section IV
How Boards See Themselves and How Their Publics See Them

CHAPTER 6

Strengthening a Grass Roots American Institution: The School Board

Jacqueline P. Danzberger and Michael D. Usdan

This chapter focuses on the substantive findings of the Institute for Educational Leadership's (IEL) 1986 report, *School Boards: Strengthening Grassroots Leadership*, and discusses the implications of those findings for local educational governance. We also describe IEL's subsequent and continuing work with state school boards associations and local boards throughout the country. In the first section, the school board, as a mechanism of representative government, is placed in the larger political context of a more centralized society in which the performance of many of the nation's basic institutions at every governmental level is under serious question. We then describe how influential new participants such as governors and business leaders have recently broadened the base of educational decision making. The bulk of the chapter is focused on IEL's extensive work for six years on school board issues. This work is first discussed in the framework of the more generic findings and implications of IEL's 1986 nationwide study. Following this discussion, major findings derived from work with school boards that participated in the 1988–89 demonstration of IEL's School Board Effectiveness Program are presented. Data are derived from a national sample of some 266 school boards in fifteen states. These data reflect board members' own assessments of their boards' effectiveness.

From these data, our national report, and our nationwide work, we shall draw implications for the future role of school boards. The look to the future stresses the general need for boards to strengthen their leadership and governance effectiveness and addresses particularly important areas for improvement such as creating linkages with general government, other children and family service agencies, and the business community; improving accountability for their governance of the schools; setting new priorities for the work of boards; and involving parents and community members in the school.

THE LARGER POLITICAL ENVIRONMENT

In many respects, local school boards are one of the last bastions of meaningful local government. As life in general and social, economic, and political conditions have become ever more complex, decision making in most government policy realms has become more centralized at the state and national levels. Local school districts have become the linchpin of communities, particularly the suburbs, which have burgeoned so dramatically since World War II. Indeed, most parents predicate their decision on whether or not to move to a particular community on the perceived quality of the school district that their children will attend. In relocating, corporations frequently predicate their decisions on the quality of school districts in a particular geographic area. The prestige of a community and the price of real estate are assessed not by the quality of the jurisdiction's police, fire, or sanitation departments, but by the reputation of its school system.

Thus, the wealthier and more politically influential citizens who live in the more prestigious districts are not apt to want to alter the governance or districting patterns of their schools. This long-cherished tradition of localism is deeply embedded in American educational and political history and tradition, in rural as well as in metropolitan areas, and helps to explain the protectionist and defensive attitudes of citizens and school boards in many school districts as the pressure for educational change escalates from state and national authorities.

An overarching theme of this chapter, borne out by the data from IEL's work with boards of education, is that school boards, the pivotal local governance mechanism for public education, frequently are isolated from much of the ferment currently being generated by the education reform movement, and from the agencies, institutions, and government bodies that have a direct impact on children and their families, and on the political environment in their communities. This relative isolation from the political mainstream and general government insulates many boards from the reform initiatives being promulgated by increasingly involved business leaders, governors, and other influentials. The lack of involvement on the part of school boards creates serious problems for advocates of enduring educational change, as we shall note in the following pages. As the IEL data discussed subsequently in this chapter reflect, there seems to be in many school jurisdictions a discontinuity between the rhetoric and strategies of the widely heralded reform movement and the attitudes and operating assumptions of many school boards that do believe they are acting as a representative governing body at the local level.

A fundamental, if rarely posed, question confronts everyone concerned with improving the decentralized public education enterprise. How can the national agenda, as articulated by the President and the governors in their unprecedented promulgation of national goals, and the visions of dramatic restructuring of schools, as espoused by influential business groups such as the Business Roundtable and the National Alliance of Business, be reconciled with the apparent satisfaction of so many citizens with their schools? School board members at the community level may, in fact, be accurately reflecting the viewpoints of the citizens who elect them, and the majority of board members, as IEL has found, believe that it is their job to do what the community wants. Indeed, in our system, elected school board officials in many, if not most, cases are representing the values of their local constituents, particularly in economically affluent and politically influential suburban districts and homogeneous rural and small-town school districts where the current education system is ostensibly working.

More systematic attention must be paid to this fundamental dilemma of representative government. The glacial tempo of educational change may not be as attributable to conservative status quo-oriented school board members as it is to the penchants of the voters who elect them, and to underlying community values and goals. The difficulty of changing existing institutions in this increasingly complex and pluralistic society is certainly not limited to education. The recent paralysis of national leadership in trying to resolve the federal budget crisis illustrates the point. We simply want to emphasize from the outset that the problems confronting reformers vis-à-vis school boards and other institutions responsible for education are symptomatic of the problem of effecting substantial change in any of the policy realms in the nation's increasingly pluralistic and issue-divided society. Numerous interest groups in every phase of public life seemingly have the power to deter change in a political system that is increasingly fractured and in gridlock. Without the support of elected local officials, enduring change or reform in public education is unlikely. It behooves all of us not to ignore or bypass school boards but to give much more scrutiny to understanding the behavior of the individuals who constitute this unique representative, grass roots institution.

BROADENED DECISION MAKING

In the past decade or so, new and influential actors have dramatically expanded their participation in the shaping of educational policy in the United States. Business leaders, governors, state legislators, and prestigious academics have paid unprecedented attention to the quality of the schools and have joined in an escalating national movement to improve the nation's education system.

Local school boards, which are ostensibly responsible for formulating local educational policy in the nation's decentralized educational system, increasingly have been bypassed or confronted with faits accomplis as consequential educational changes have been suggested by hundreds of influential and broadly based blue ribbon commissions and implemented by governors and state legislatures throughout the country.

Among the basic premises of IEL's 1986 study was the notion that school boards had been largely ignored in the early years of the education reform process and that this reality did not augur well for chances of sustaining the national reform movement's momentum nor for the implementation of education reforms. The local school board is a unique American grass roots institution with approximately ninety-seven thousand board members (95 percent of whom are elected) having policymaking responsibilities for some fifteen thousand local school districts. With the exception of Canada (where there are strong provincial ministries of education along with local boards), the other industrialized nations have national education systems with central ministries of education both setting and implementing policy and administrative practices.

The IEL study was predicated on the assumption that if local boards remained uninvolved and uninformed, then implementing the reforms would be difficult, and indeed there would be no national impetus to improve local governance if boards continued to be left out of the policy debates. School boards retain important decision-making prerogatives in the nation's decentralized educational governance structure. They possess the power to hire and fire the superintendent and other key personnel, have the ultimate budgetary responsibility, and set policy parameters in a wide spectrum of school matters. School boards set the tone for the district, and their support is essential if efforts to "restructure" schools and schooling through school-site management and creation of strong community linkages are to be implemented successfully.

The first years of school reform in the early and mid 1980s focused on state-level legislative and regulatory initiatives designed to increase student achievement through the imposition of higher academic standards (requirements to take more courses in certain curriculum areas) and more rigorous testing requirements for both teachers and students. In the late 1980s, attention began to focus on "restructuring" the locus of decision making in school districts (school-site management) and broadening parental and community involvement in the schools. This reflected the growing conviction of reformers that centralized mandates would not be successful and that significant improvement would occur only through approaches that stressed school site-based initiatives to enlarge the decision-making prerogatives of teachers, parents, and principals at the building level. In other words, the contradiction between the widespread acceptance of the effective schools research focusing on the pivotal role of the building level in education improvement and centralized regulations and standardization became readily apparent. Thus, the ongoing education reform debate has emphasized either "top-down" state regulations and prescriptions or "bottom-up" building-level initiatives. The crucial district level of school governance, at which local school boards and superintendents function, has been somewhat ignored and "sandwiched" into a largely passive role. Rightly or wrongly, local boards to some extent and their superintendents, strategically placed at the nexus between the individual schools and the state, have been commonly viewed by reformers as being part of the problem and not integral to the solution of the nation's perceived crisis in public education.

IEL's 1986 STUDY

IEL's aforementioned national study in 1986 was designed to focus attention on school boards as corporate governing bodies. Data were collected from over four hundred school board chairs in nine major Standard Metropolitan Areas (SMA's): Hartford (Connecticut), Washington, D.C., Atlanta, Dallas-Ft. Worth, the San Francisco Bay Area, Denver, Indianapolis, Columbus (Ohio), and Pittsburgh. Nine case studies were carried out in larger school districts (ten thousand or more students) in each of the areas, and more than three hundred interviews were conducted with various individuals in each of the nine SMA's. All board members in the nine case study districts were also surveyed. Questionnaires were also sent to rural school boards in Idaho, Iowa, and Wyoming.

The study's purposes were to project the school board more visibly into the ongoing public debate and dialogue about educational reform. The hope was that a candid analysis of the strengths and weaknesses of the American school board by an impartial outside group would strengthen chances for enduring reform by insinuating the crucial role of school boards more forcefully into the national discussion of school governance and education reform policy.

It became readily apparent that the growing numbers of education-oriented governors, legislators, business and civic leaders, and others who had become involved in the reform initiatives of the 1980s were not going to attack school boards frontally or explicitly seek to curb their legal authority. These influential reformers often were critical of the passivity and lack of leadership of boards and largely ignored or bypassed state school boards associations and local boards in conceptualizing and enacting their reform initiatives. Although school boards frequently were viewed as dysfunctional defenders of the status quo and not particularly well disposed to supporting reform efforts, there were no serious attempts made either to eliminate local school boards or to curb their existing powers. Indeed, with all the rhetoric by influential governors, business and civic leaders, and the countless recommendations promulgated by hundreds of "blue ribbon" study commissions all over the country, which were so critical of those responsible for governing the "failing" schools, virtually no specific suggestions were made either to infringe on the legal authority or to recast the institutional role of the school board. However, erosions of local control did occur. States have become, for instance, much more prescriptive and intrusive in curriculum, student and teacher testing, and promotion policies, areas historically sacred to local control. The major power shift has occurred in who pays the bill for K–12 public education. States in the early 1980s became the dominant provider of education funding.

As the IEL study team collected information for its 1986 book and interviewed political, business and civic, and educational leaders throughout the country, we began to understand the reasons why the school board was not more frontally or openly assaulted by the reformers. The team discovered that there was a great deal of "grass roots" support for school boards as an important mechanism for representative government. Local elected boards dealt with two of the most important elements in citizens' lives—their children and tax dollars. Citizens were reluctant, irrespective of how they perceived their own school boards, to lose local access to and control of those responsible for shaping policy on these singularly important matters. Citizens also perceived the school board as a "buffer" between the community and professional educators.

In other words, school boards, despite their weaknesses and the criticisms heaped on them locally, have been part of the essential "warp and woof" of the representative governance fabric in communities throughout the country. Politically sensitive governors and legislators, cognizant of this reality and the serious political repercussions they might face, have been reluctant to challenge overtly the basic educational governance structure, with its reliance on local school boards. When the IEL team suggested to interviewees other possible structures or asked for possible governance alternatives, there was consensus that the existing school board structure, even with its imperfections, should be maintained. Other options such as centralized state control or professional hegemony without lay involvement were negatively regarded. Local lay control through a vehicle like school boards was considered essential to the survival of public education. Respondents felt that the schools were too important to be left exclusively in the hands of the professionals and that schools needed lay control. Too much centralization and standardization at the state level would deprive parents of access to those responsible for their children's education and would further erode middle-class support for public schools. Mayors and city council members interviewed were not eager to assume responsibility for education governance.

This grass roots support for the school board, however, is somewhat paradoxical. As journalist Neal Peirce stated in his preface to the IEL study (1986, p. iv), "This report throws sudden and welcome light on that dark island of American governance, the institution that everyone knows of but few understand: the school board." Peirce's point was corroborated in the IEL study. Although interviewees in the study and others may support the school board structure vis-à-vis other possible governance arrangements, very few respondents, including rather sophisticated and civically engaged citizens, know very much about the role and responsibilities of local school boards. Most Americans are only episodically involved with the schools, and their knowledge tends to be anecdotal. Many parents, for example, certainly are engaged with the PTAs, teachers, and administrators in the schools their children attend, but they have very little knowledge or interest in the school system itself or in the respective roles and the responsibilities of the school board or the school superintendent. The problem is further compounded by the reality that less than one-quarter of the nation's households currently have school-age children.

This civic illiteracy about school boards has widespread ramifications. The public indifference or apathy is certainly reflected in the abysmally low voter turnout that characterizes most school board elections. It is not uncommon, for example, to have only 5 to 15 percent of the eligible voters participate in school board elections, which in most states are held at different times during the year than the more publicized general elections at which presidents, governors, senators, congressmen, state legislators, mayors, and city councilmen are elected. Most states have removed school boards from the political party structure. While historically well-intentioned, this has reinforced school boards' isolation and lack of political clout, according to many who were interviewed.

The sparse turnout at school board elections, of course, makes it easier for small special interest groups to determine the outcome. In most communities, small groups of organized voters with vested interests or particular "axes to grind" can control who wins the school board election. This often creates problems, since candidates frequently run against incumbent board members and school district administrators. Tension then often develops on the newly constituted board between new members and the remaining members of the "old guard," whom the new members may have attacked during the election campaign. A board's effectiveness and public image as an informed and deliberative governing body is often weakened by such internal conflicts.

Elections with small voter turnouts and dominated by special-interest or single-issue groups also have tended to erode the "trustee" concept of membership, through which board members view themselves as representing the entire community and not just a narrow constituency or the interest group that helped to elect them. This problem was frequently cited to the IEL team as a major reason why the caliber of school board members in many communities is perceived to have changed. Many influential and respected citizens reportedly are reluctant to serve as board members because of the seemingly endless and often petty controversies that engulf the schools and the boards. When committed people are elected to boards, they can quickly become frustrated as they are swept up in a variety of volatile issues that frequently have little or nothing to do with the formulation and implementation of educational policy. Board members, or the board as a whole, are frequently expected by their constituencies to make decisions that are not within their purview. Many citizens do not understand the differences and nuances between the role and authority of school boards and those of professional administrators. In addition, most citizens (and many board members) do not understand that individual board members have no legal authority, that authority is vested in the actions of the board as a corporate entity.

As controversial societal issues such as desegregation, finance, church-state relationships, collective bargaining, sex education, and AIDS have impinged on the schools, local district leadership commonly has become enmeshed in a host of complex problems spilling into the schools from problems in the larger society. These realities and the attendant frustrations have made it increasingly difficult to attract candidates to serve on school boards. The demands of school board service have caused tremendous turnover among board members, and it is not unusual for the composition of boards to reflect a 20 to 30 percent annual turnover. This lack of continuity on boards has served to weaken the school board as an institution and diminish its state and national influence. A school board with its membership constantly changing has difficulty in fully comprehending the complexities of the school district that it is responsible for governing, and in providing coherent policy direction.

The IEL study indicated that many boards had serious problems relating to their governing, policy-setting, and operational responsibilities. Boards as corporate bodies and individual members themselves were often perceived to lack management, interpersonal, and leadership skills. Although these criticisms of boards are not very different from those directed to other publicly elected or appointed government bodies, the IEL study revealed that public expectations of school officials appear to be higher and anger keener when school boards do not manage or lead well.

Many highly motivated school board members who are concerned primarily with education find themselves subjected to the constant glare of publicity and media attention. They frequently are unaccustomed to living a "fishbowl" existence and, unlike many of their counterparts in general government, do not relish being public figures. Often, they are frustrated by their limited influence within the education sphere and disillusioned with the fact that so much of their limited time is spent on inconsequential, ministerial details that have very little connection to their important educational policy responsibilities. However, despite their frustrations about how boards spend their time and concerns about their effectiveness, board members interviewed in the study had few concrete suggestions for improving the situation.

School board members confront unique responsibilities, since they serve as both corporate managers and elected officials in the governance structure for public education. Many critics of school boards feel that the boards are mired in inconsequential detail and are not fulfilling their policy role, and they believe that boards should be restructured to resemble the more detached corporate board model—meeting less frequently, limiting public access to their deliberations, and being concerned with only major educational policy issues. In other words, school board members should spend less time worrying about whether the buses are running on time or the buns are hot in the cafeteria, and be more concerned with how teachers are deployed and the curriculum devised to enhance student learning and academic outcomes. Most observers of the American educational scene, however, do not believe that the corporate school board model would work. Schools, unlike private corporations, are simply too public, visible, and suffused with politically related issues. When dealing with people's children, taxes, and deeply held and often conflicting community values at the local level, wide public access and extensive participation simply cannot be foreclosed.

The tradition of grass roots involvement in school affairs is deeply embedded in the nation's political culture, and school boards persist as very basic institutions in the national education governance structure and tradition. This history and established tradition pose a major challenge to advocates of educational change—a challenge that continues to be singularly ignored by most policymakers and reformers. This generally ignored challenge is how to strengthen the governing skills and shape a more appropriate and viable policymaking role for the citizens who serve on school boards throughout the country. The IEL study documented the need to develop frameworks and programs for local boards of education to improve their leadership and operational effectiveness. In other words, boards need to engage in self-evaluation and developmental activities to improve their effectiveness. This demonstrated need precipitated the development of IEL's School Board Effectiveness Program, which was developed and nationally demonstrated in cooperation with the National School Boards Association and fourteen state school boards associations throughout the country. This program will be discussed later in this chapter. The following section presents some of the important findings from the 1986 study.

FINDINGS FROM THE 1986 STUDY

The study confirmed general support for the fundamental role of local boards and belief among citizens of the importance of grass roots lay leadership for public education. But, many concerns were articulated by the boards, citizens, and professional employees of case study school districts about the shortcomings of boards and the need to strengthen their capacity to govern in an era of great dissatisfaction with American education and increasingly complex needs of students. The following summarizes some of the major issues identified in the IEL study.

The chairs of local boards in the study sample attested to the common complaint that boards spend too much of their time dealing with administrative trivia and too little time on major substantive concerns such as the quality of the education program and student learning outcomes. Respondents also expressed concern about the diminished trusteeship concept of board service and the growing number of special interest representatives who seek election to boards and often use involvement with schools as a political stepping stone. Such behavior increasingly exacerbated interpersonal tension on boards and made it difficult for the members to function effectively as a corporate body. Many boards behaved poorly in public and did not know how to disagree amicably or resolve conflicts that were affecting a board's work. As a result, their image frequently suffered and the reputation of the public schools in the community was further diminished.

As mentioned earlier, there is an elusive but definite sense that school board service is not attracting the civic and business leaders who have political influence as it once did in many communities. In the urban school districts particularly, there is a perceived loss of access to civic power bases as influential citizens, for a variety of reasons, opt not to serve on local school boards. Many persons interviewed for the study felt that the pipeline of talented and influential community volunteers who might have served on local boards in the past is closing down as highly educated women, in particular, pursue paid jobs in business and the professions. The plus side of the change is that urban boards are more representative of the diversity in these school districts.

School boards from urban and changing school districts faced a growing problem as the political constituency of the schools shrank and the student population became increasingly minority, economically disadvantaged, and politically disenfranchised. With less than 25 percent of the households in the country having children enrolled in public schools, the political muscle of older, more affluent citizens was viewed as expanding at the expense of the clients of the schools.

This critically important erosion of education's political base of support poses new challenges and possibly new roles for educational leaders. Under the assumption that elected officials likely will respond to the money and influence of older voters, it may well be necessary for school board leaders to devote more attention to building new coalitions with business leaders and other groups. The growing interest in education being manifested by the business community should be welcomed by school board members. The private sector has begun to recognize that the nation's economic survival in an increasingly competitive international economy will depend on the capacity of the schools to produce a capable workforce. Business leaders are beginning to recognize that investments in education are not just philanthropy but are manifestations of enlightened self-interest. The inextricable link between education and the economy is the handle through which business and other politically essential support can be mustered to assist the schools. School boards should be more pro-active and less passive in the creation of new, more broadly gauged coalitions to buttress education.

A number of other important issues relating to school boards were identified by respondents to the IEL questionnaire and interviewees in the nine case study districts. The continuing issue of board-superintendent relationships was often cited. In many systems, there was an incessant need to distinguish between the board of education's policymaking prerogatives and the school superintendent's adminis-trative responsibilities. We found that there frequently was conflict when the lines of demarcation between policy and administration were too precisely delineated. There were fewer problems in situations in which the ambiguities and gray areas were acknowledged and mutual trust and candor prevailed in board-superintendent rela-tionships.

Problems with the media also were articulated by many board members who cited their frustration with newspaper and television coverage that stressed only the negative. They were annoyed that in major metropolitan areas with literally hundreds of schools, the widely watched nightly prime time newscast would focus only on the individual school in which a fight, strike, boycott, or like incident might have occurred. This problem is particularly serious in major urban areas where the seemingly intractable problems of the core city school systems dominate media attention.

This type of "sensationalized" negative coverage of school issues gives the entire education enterprise a poor public image and frus-trates board members. These problems with the media that were and are found throughout the country could be mitigated if more board members began to work vigorously to cultivate important broader external constituencies such as the media. Boards, instead of being passive and reacting only after negative stories are reported, should be more proactive in seeking meetings with editors and editorial boards in efforts to explain school issues and problems. It is too late once the story breaks. Greater understanding and sensitivity to complex edu-cational problems can be generated by informal discussions prior to the emergence of a crisis. School boards exhibit a tendency to defer too frequently to their superintendents and administrative staffs in nurturing external constituencies such as the media. Superintendents usually are not indigenous to the community and frequently serve only three- to four-year terms. Administrators do not have the roots or long-standing ties in the community possessed by many board members. Indeed, superintendents are relatively transient and usually do not have the time or opportunity to build the requisite political base with the media, senior citizens, the civic and business leadership, and other groups external to the school system. Thus, it may again be incumbent on board members in many districts to redirect their priorities and spend less time on day-to-day internal school issues and more time with the external constituencies on which the educational system will increasingly depend. Indeed, demographic and political realities cited earlier compel such a reassessment of the school board's role.

The need for board members to adopt a broader conception of the board's role is reflected in the changes that have occurred in state-local district relationships in recent years. Board chairs in the survey and board members in the case study districts cited time and again the centralization that was occurring as state governors, legislatures, and education departments assumed more direct authority over public education. In numerous states, new statutes and regulations imposed many requirements and constraints on the prerogatives of local boards. As discussed earlier, local officials were rarely consulted as these policies were conceptualized and enacted. This lack of consultation was understandably resented by local school boards and superintendents who felt ignored and bypassed. Most importantly, however, these state-level changes reflected governors', legislators', business leaders', and other influentials' lack of confidence in school boards and educators at the local level. Many boards in the study said they had initiated reforms themselves in areas of state-legislated reforms. Boards expressed concern that many state reforms were designed to bring poorer districts up to minimal educational standards and that many of these reforms were well below what the better districts were already doing. They stated that some state mandates such as state requirements for norm-referenced tests rather than criterion-referenced tests were actually forcing their boards into regressive positions.

This trend toward centralizing education at the state level quite understandably has generated considerable tension between local and state educational authorities. The tendency of states to regulate and to interfere with local districts (called "Big Foot" metaphorically in the IEL report), reflects the aforementioned inconsistencies or contradictions between state control as emphasized in the early years of the reform movement and the "effective schools," "school-site management" thrust espoused by reformers in more recent years. It is relevant to emphasize again that school boards and other established officials at the district level often have been either ignored or bypassed in these dichotomous "top-down" or "bottom-up" modes of school reform.

Indeed, a persuasive case can be made that boards and superintendents are sandwiched between state directives and school-site initiatives that focus on more autonomy for teachers, principals, and parents. There is an urgent need for increased local-state dialogue. School boards are uniquely positioned as intermediaries to broker the discussions that must occur between state and building-level educational officials and policymakers.

IEL's objectives for the 1986 study were to produce a report that would be both informative about the condition of local boards and helpful in providing guidance for board improvement to school boards and the state school boards associations.

To meet the latter objective, the study team developed a framework of fifteen indicators of school board effectiveness. These indicators addressed the spectrum of major school board roles and responsibilities and incorporated the major areas of concern about school boards' performance from the study findings. Following publication of the report, these fifteen indicators were further refined (as stated below) and became the framework of the school board self-assessment instrument for IEL's School Board Effectiveness Program.

The Indicators of School Board Effectiveness

An effective board

I. provides leadership for public education and is an advocate for the educational needs and interests of children and youth.

II. seeks and responds to many forms of parent and community participation in the school system.

III. has a comprehensive program for communications with its various constituencies, including policies and procedures for working with the media.

IV. works to influence policies of state and local governmental bodies and other organizations whose decisions affect children and youth.

V. encourages and respects diversity, deals openly and straightforwardly with controversy within the board and the community, and follows democratic decision-making procedures.

VI. uses strategic planning to set educational goals and determine the means for accomplishing them.

VII. works to ensure an adequate flow of resources and achieves equity in their distribution.

VIII. establishes and follows policy to govern its own policymaking responsibilities.

IX. exercises continuing policy oversight of education programs and their management, drawing information for this purpose from many sources and knowing enough to ask the right questions.

X. establishes and implements procedures for selecting and evaluating the superintendent.

XI. recognizes the dilemma of distinguishing policy from administration and periodically clarifies these separate areas in consultation with the superintendent.

XII. promotes constructive relations with its employees and works to create conditions that enhance productivity.

XIII. establishes clear expectations for the conduct of its members.

XIV. establishes and follows policies and procedures to manage its own operations.

XV. has procedures for self-assessment and invests in its own development, using diverse approaches that address the needs of the board as a whole, as well as those of individual board members.

THE SCHOOL BOARD EFFECTIVENESS PROGRAM

This section provides a brief description of the development of the components of the School Board Effectiveness Program, and it provides background for the ensuing discussion of some important findings from the self-assessment data of the school boards that participated in the national program demonstration in 1988 and 1989.

Boards in the 1986 study confirmed what the IEL study team and others perceived—few school boards were conducting any kind of self-assessment, and those that were found it difficult to act on the results of their own assessments. A survey of assessment instruments available to school boards produced no truly comprehensive instrument with an array of assessment items addressing specific individual actions or behaviors from which a board could plan specific improvements.

IEL had two major objectives in initiating the program:

1. To develop a self-assessment system that provided for comprehensive self-assessment and incorporated strategies to help boards act on the results of their assessments.
2. To promote widespread board self-assessment and follow-up development activities to improve school board effectiveness.

In order to facilitate achievement of both these objectives, the development of the program became a cooperative effort between IEL and the state school boards association community. State associations provide approximately 95 percent of all development/informational activities for local school board members and boards. Exceptions to this dependency on the state associations occur among boards of large urban and "lighthouse" suburban school districts.

Nine state associations have been involved with IEL from the inception of program development (Arizona, Connecticut, Illinois, Kentucky, Michigan, New Jersey, New York, Virginia, and Wyoming). Five state associations subsequently joined in the national program demonstration (New Hampshire, West Virginia, Iowa, Wisconsin, and Minnesota). Through a program for urban boards of the Danforth Foundation of St. Louis (the original funder of the IEL program), several urban boards in California and Texas also participated in the national demonstration.

The program, as has been stated, is based on findings from the 1986 study and uses the indicators framework for board self-assessment. The program takes a board from self-assessment through to a written Improvement Plan. All board members anonymously complete the fifteen section Board Effectiveness Inventory (the self-assessment instrument). Members' responses are aggregated into a Board Effectiveness Profile (the report to a board). A facilitator trained in the program and in group facilitation works with a board to discuss assessment findings, set priorities for board improvement, and develop a written improvement plan. Program materials developed also include a Board Improvement Planning Guide and a Facilitator Guide. IEL has also developed a "board-administered" option for the self-assessment and improvement planning process that does not require a facilitator. This option is not recommended for boards with internal conflicts or where there is board-superintendent conflict.

In 1989 and early 1990, development of the full School Board Effectiveness Program was completed with the creation and field-testing of five Board Development Modules. Topics for these modules are Setting Norms and Expectations for Board Members; Board/Superintendent Relations; the Local Board and Community Involvement; Planning and Goal Setting; and Policy Oversight.

The topics reflect areas of greatest perceived need for improvement among boards in the national demonstration and areas for which IEL's state association partners defined greatest need for new, creative development materials.

The following section explains the self-assessment instrument, assessment rating scale, and how the self-assessment data are presented to boards.

The Board Effectiveness Inventory and the Board Effectiveness Profile

It is important to be familiar with the self-assessment instrument in order to interpret findings from the national data. As indicated earlier, the instrument has fifteen sections corresponding to the fifteen indicators of school board effectiveness. Within each section, members of a board individually rate anywhere from eight to fifteen specific assessment items. A six-point rating scale is used, which asks a board member to rate the degree of his or her *agreement* with the statement in terms of the board on which the respondent serves. The agreement scale is used for fourteen of fifteen sections. The assessment items for Indicator IV, Influencing Others, ask a board member, on a six-point rating scale, to assess how active the board is for each assessment item. Table 6.1 provides a sample section of the instrument.

Completed self-assessment instruments from all board members are then scored and the mean score for the board for each assessment item is produced, as well as a mean score for each of the fifteen sections. This mean for each of the fifteen sections is produced from the board's mean scores for each assessment item in each section. A Board Effectiveness Profile (the report to the board) is then prepared,

Table 6.1
Sample Section of the Board Effectiveness Inventory

IX. Policy Oversight: An effective board exercises continuing policy oversight of education programs and their management, drawing information for this purpose from many sources and knowing enough to ask the right questions.

Our Board:	Strongly Disagree	Moderately Disagree	Slightly Disagree	Slightly Agree	Moderately Agree	Strongly Agree
1. Has procedures for board oversight of education policies and programs.	1	2	3	4	5	6
2. Allows sufficient time for the review of education policies and programs.	1	2	3	4	5	6
3. Uses outcome measures (indicators) to assess progress toward the goals and objectives of the school district.	1	2	3	4	5	6
4. Uses outcome measures (indicators) to assess the progress of each school toward its goals and objectives.	1	2	3	4	5	6
5. Monitors expenditures to ensure conformity with the budget.	1	2	3	4	5	6
6. Has procedures to ensure timely and well-organized information on policy implementation.	1	2	3	4	5	6
7. Has information systems to monitor board policies and program implementation.	1	2	3	4	5	6

8. List the two or three important problems and challenges your board faces in exercising policy oversight. *Use the space provided in the enclosed Answer Booklet.*

Anytown, U.S.A. School Board
IX. Policy Oversight
Distribution of Ratings

giving the board a chart with its ratings for each item in each section, including the number of board members that gave a particular rating to each item. In addition to the charts with the mean scores, a three-column chart is prepared for each section, which helps guide a board to consider the results of its self-assessment in terms of where the scores show the board believes it is not very effective, where scores indicate that the board is slightly to somewhat effective and needs to discuss its performance, and where the board feels it is generally effective. (See Tables 6.2 and 6.3 for sample charts.)

IEL's philosophy about board self-assessment is that the process of the self-assessment exercise is in itself a developmental activity for the board and that the assessment results should not be treated as a score card, that is, we pass at this score, we fail at that score. The results of a board self-assessment should help the board determine where it needs to improve; should provide a framework for all board members to discuss their perceptions about areas of concern and where board members believe they are performing well, adequately, or poorly; and should guide a board in setting priorities for its improvement. Through confronting major role and responsibility behaviors and outcomes that are affecting the board's ability to govern, the satisfaction of all board members with the work of the board should improve along with the community's and school district's perceptions about the board.

Self-assessment confirms effectiveness and helps identify, through assessment results and discussion, where attention needs to be paid to performance. Comments about the self-assessment instrument from boards in the national demonstration confirmed that for many board members and the boards as a whole, this was the first time they had considered at one time the range of their boards' responsibilities and their actions and behaviors within these responsibilities.

FINDINGS FROM THE DATA: PERFORMANCE OF BOARDS IN THE IEL NATIONAL DEMONSTRATION SAMPLE

The Sample

Data have been analyzed from a sample of 266 boards and 130 superintendents. Not all state associations in the demonstration had

Table 6.2

Sample Chart Showing Distribution of Ratings on Seven Items Relating to Policy Oversight

Assessment Items	1	2	3	4	5	6	Total	Mean
1. Has procedures for oversight of policies and programs			1	5		2	8	4.4
2. Allows time for review of policies and programs			1	3	2	2	8	4.6
3. Uses indicators to assess progress toward objectives	1	2	1	2	2		8	3.3
4. Uses indicators to assess achievement of school goals	1	2		3	1	1	8	3.5
5. Monitors expenditures to conform with budget					3	6	9	5.7
6. Ensures timely information on policy implementation				2	3	2	7	5.0
7. Has information systems to monitor policies/programs			2	3	1	1	7	4.1

1=Strongly disagree
2=Moderately disagree
3=Slightly disagree
4=Slightly agree
5=Moderately agree
6=Strongly agree

Table 6.3
Sample Chart Showing Ratings of Overall Effectiveness on Seven Items Relating to Policy Oversight

IX. Policy Oversight

Our Board:	Not Very Effective (1.0–4.0)	Somewhat Effective (4.1–5.0)	Generally Effective (5.1–6.0)
1. Has procedures for board oversight of education policies and programs.			
2. Allows sufficient time for the review of education policies and programs.		✓	
3. Uses outcome measures (indicators) to assess progress toward the goals and objectives of the school district.	✓	✓	
4. Uses outcome measures (indicators) to assess the progress of each school toward its goals and objectives.	✓		
5. Monitors expenditures to ensure conformity within the budget.			✓
6. Has procedures to ensure timely and well-organized information on policy implementation.		✓	
7. Has information systems to monitor board policies and program implementation.		✓ *	

* At least two board members disagree at some level.

the superintendents of their demonstration boards complete an instrument. Where superintendents did participate, their results were, of course, kept separate from the boards' and were known only to the facilitators working with a board.

The sample includes 75 suburban boards, 70 urban boards, and 121 rural/small town boards. Except for the Virginia boards in the sample, all other boards are elected. There are county boards, boards of consolidated districts, and boards of K–8 and high school districts. Most of the boards in the sample govern school districts contiguous with city/town boundaries.

Boards self-selected into the demonstration program. However, IEL requested that the participating state associations include in their sample group of boards some boards that were experiencing difficulties.

The Findings

We stated earlier that board self-assessment should be viewed not as a report card, but as a tool to guide board improvement and reinforce successes, and now we ask the reader to bring that philosophy to his or her reactions to the discussion of these boards' assessment data.

These boards, across all fifteen indicators, gave themselves a 4.52 rating on a 6.0 scale—they slightly to moderately agreed that their boards evidenced the actions and behaviors stated in all the assessment items. The superintendents in the sample gave their boards a 4.91 rating across the fifteen indicators. This would seem to run counter to the common thinking about how superintendents view their boards. Two phenomena may be at work in this finding: (1) the superintendents in the sample were concerned that despite all precautions, their assessments would fall into the hands of their boards, and/or (2) superintendents identify their own performance with that of their boards. A third possibility is that board members, when given the opportunity to assess anonymously the performance of their boards, are more critical of themselves than we suspect. The chart in Table 6.4 displays the self-assessment data for each indicator, giving the ratings for all boards, and for boards in urban, suburban, and rural/small town school districts, and the last column displays the superintendents' ratings.

Discussion of these data, and of data presented later in this section for some individual assessment items, is presented with the following

Table 6.4
Ratings from 266 Boards of Education and 130 Superintendents on Fifteen Indicators of School Board Effectiveness

Indicators*	All Boards N = 266	Urban N = 70	Suburban N = 75	Rural/Small Town N = 121	All Superintendents N = 130
I. Leadership	4.57	4.41	4.64	4.62	4.72
II. Parent and Community Involvement	4.35	4.27	5.07	4.06	4.6
III. Communications	4.67	4.49	4.85	4.75	4.9
IV. Influence on Others	3.46	3.88	3.25	3.42	3.3
V. Decision Making	4.98	4.56	5.07	5.83	4.97
VI. Planning and Goal Setting	4.52	4.3	4.72	4.61	4.64
VII. Resource Allocation	4.8	4.8	5.07	4.8	5.06
VIII. Policy Development	4.78	4.62	4.92	4.4	5.07
IX. Policy Oversight	4.27	4.0	4.44	4.45	4.57
X. Selection and Evaluation of the Superintendent	4.68	4.62	4.86	4.76	4.94
XI. Working with the Superintendent	4.86	4.59	4.92	4.49	4.89
XII. Employee Relations	4.88	4.77	4.98	4.97	5.03
XIII. Expectations for Board Member Conduct	4.55	4.52	4.67	5.13	4.95
XIV. Board Operations	4.63	4.41	4.66	4.71	4.98
XV. Board Development	3.87	3.47	3.97	4.0	4.05

* Abbreviations for the indicators are used. Please refer to the list of the indicators on pages 105–106 for the full indicator statements.

caveat: The differences among ratings in assessment items by the full sample and by suburban, urban, and rural/small town boards for many of the indicators are not statistically significant, but they do indicate some areas in which boards feel they are less effective than in others. The discussion of the data focuses on those areas of significance in the context of the national educational reform agenda and growing questions about the effective functioning of local school boards. We believe these data, despite some limitations, do provide useful and revealing information about school boards.

A compelling finding from these data is that irrespective of how different their school districts and community environments may be, urban, suburban, and rural/small town boards reflect remarkable unanimity in their assessments of their performance. Urban boards' ratings are somewhat lower overall than ratings for the full sample, but among the five indicators with the lowest ratings by the full sample, urban and rural boards have four indicators in common, and all boards have three of these indicators in common.

The uniformity among our data for all boards was even more striking when the three categories of boards' ratings for individual assessment items in each of the fifteen indicators were analyzed. The two or three lowest-rated assessment items in each of the fifteen sections of the instrument were the same for each of the three categories of boards.

IEL's 1986 study found many more similarities than differences among boards across types of communities. These board self-assessment data from the national program demonstration sample confirm the earlier findings, but provide much greater specificity about the nature of the issues that determine the effectiveness of local boards of education.

A complete analysis of all the data is obviously not feasible in this chapter. The following summary focuses on highlights from the data that are of particular significance in the context of current general critiques of the effectiveness of school boards in promoting education reform and improvement in their school districts. Using the self-assessment rating scale, we have defined a rating below 5.0 (moderate agreement with an assessment item) as an indication of less than desired performance by the boards.

The Functioning Board

The boards' data indicate concerns about effectiveness in several aspects of boards' communications functions—absence of policies for relating with the media, having effective strategies for communicating with groups in their communities, providing opportunities in the community for discussion of educational issues, seeking views from the community about the performance of the schools, sharing progress toward the school districts' and schools' goals and objectives with the community, and having policies for boards' communications with district employees and with constituents.

The capacity of school board members to make informed decisions through skilled group decision-making processes is critical to boards' functioning effectively. Urban and suburban boards in our sample indicated they needed to improve in their decision-making skills, and all three categories of boards indicated there was room for improvement in the area of making board decisions based on public, not private, informal discussions. Findings from the data reveal problems in developing a common view of the role of the board among board members (a major problem for the urban boards in the sample). The data indicate that effective decision making among the boards is affected by members' lack of necessary skills to resolve interpersonal conflicts among members and less than total commitment among members in seeking to resolve interpersonal conflicts. In these latter two assessment items, the urban boards in the sample rated themselves almost a full point lower than the suburban boards.

The effectiveness of school boards is in large measure determined by the character of the board-superintendent relationship. This is an era of high turnover among superintendents, particularly in urban school districts. There are some key assessment findings that have direct bearing on this relationship and very possibly on the potential for a reasonable length of tenure for superintendents. Again, of the three board categories, urban boards rated themselves lowest in these items. Data show that the boards need to develop processes for managing board-superintendent conflicts and make greater efforts to avoid involvement in administration of their districts. The boards' data reveal that evaluations of their superintendents do not consistently reflect agreed-on performance objectives nor do boards give themselves high ratings for looking at the board-superintendent relationship as part of the superintendent's evaluation.

All boards rated themselves below 4.0 (slightly agree with an assessment item statement) in assessing boards' use of their time, having an annual calendar to plan the major work of the board, and providing a comprehensive and effective orientation for new board members. The urban boards rated themselves at 3.6 for devoting adequate attention and time to education programs and educational outcomes. The rural/small town and suburban boards rated themselves just slightly higher in this critical use of boards' time.

The growing complexity of the roles and responsibilities of school boards and the challenges of providing quality education to an increasingly diverse student population are likely to exacerbate these findings about how boards function as governing bodies in the future. Performance in just three of the assessment items discussed above—having a common view of the role of the board, possessing skills to resolve interpersonal conflicts, and working to resolve interpersonal conflicts among board members—can determine whether a school board is functioning effectively or ineffectively.

Boards and Education Reform

In the 1986 study, school boards evidenced serious concern and frustration with their having been "shut out" from a major role in shaping states' education reform agendas and regulations. On the other hand, many state policymakers, when queried, evidenced their belief that boards were part of the problem and therefore could not be part of the solution for education's ills. In the years since IEL's report was issued in 1986, states have continued developing reform agendas, and national "school board watchers" have produced very direct critiques of school board functioning and of their capacity, as currently constituted, to provide leadership for and implementation of education reforms in school districts. Criticism is particularly sharp of the more politicized boards of the nation's troubled urban school districts.

Self-assessment data from the 266 boards in IEL's sample confirm that boards view themselves as somewhat less than effective in areas critical to meeting demands on boards for education reform and greater accountability.

The increasingly complex needs of children and youth in the cities and poor rural areas require collaboration and cooperation between schools and other human services to improve educational outcomes for students. Yet, all boards assessed themselves the lowest in Indicator IV, which addresses whether a board is active in working with and influencing external communities of influence and sectors whose decisions have a direct bearing on services to children and their families, support for public education, and the creation of linkages with schools to improve the education program. Urban boards in the sample rated themselves in the ineffective rating range (2.7–3.0) for links with local human services agencies, business, and foundations, and rated themselves only slightly better (3.5) on meeting regularly with local government and on creating partnerships with business (4.0). Rural and suburban boards' assessments for these items were in the same range as the urban boards.

These findings about the relative isolation of school boards and their districts confirm one of the major findings from IEL's earlier national study in regard to boards and community leaders' perceptions about the isolation of school boards.

Improving accountability for schools, school districts, and educational governance generally is high on the national education reform agenda. Boards in the sample did not rate themselves highly overall on the assessment items in Indicator IX, Policy Oversight, nor on specific assessment items in other indicators related to having adequate information systems and school district performance measures. For example, urban boards' ratings fall between slightly disagree and slightly agree for their boards' using outcome measures to assess their systems' and schools' progress toward district goals and objectives, having adequate information systems to monitor board policies and program implementation, and allowing sufficient time for the oversight of education policies and programs. Suburban and rural/small town boards answered only slightly more positively for these items.

In the Policy Development Indicator, urban boards' assessments fall between slightly disagree and slightly agree for whether their boards define expected outcomes and accountability measures when adopting policies and programs. Communicating high expectations for all students is key to raising educational achievement and directly related to perceptions among staff of the standards for which they are accountable. The urban and suburban boards only slightly agreed that they were communicating such expectations.

Another major stream in education reform is increasing overall input of parents and the community, particularly in determining goals and objectives for school districts, and for schools. All boards in the sample rated themselves below 4.5 (only slightly agreed) in considering community input, when appropriate, to create or revise policies. Boards rated themselves somewhat lower (4.1) for involving the public and school district staff in defining criteria when selecting a new superintendent. Boards gave themselves the same rating for involving parents in setting goals and planning for individual schools. Again, the urban boards rated themselves slightly lower than the other boards in the sample for all assessment items concerning parental and community input.

Overall, the self-assessment data define many crucial areas of boards' roles and responsibilities and specific policies and behaviors to which these boards in the sample need to pay attention. And yet, the boards' assessment of their effectiveness for the items in Indicator XV, Board Development, were second lowest among the fifteen indicators. Again, these data are consistent with IEL's findings from the 1986 study. The data show that all boards in the sample gave themselves low (2.9) ratings for having annual planning retreats, and only slightly higher ratings (3.3) for assessing board performance regularly, using input from the superintendent in assessing board performance, and taking action to improve board performance if a board does assess its performance. Finally, and perhaps most tellingly, these boards slightly disagreed (3.1 rating) that their boards set aside time to learn about current national educational issues.

School boards are, by virtue of their statutory role in the educational governance structure and their direct accountability to voters, in the logical position to take the lead in creating strong support for public education and for bridging between local citizens and state and national education reformers. Our data indicate, however, that school boards, no matter how well intentioned, need to improve their performance in some key areas if they are to be taken seriously as leaders for education reform.

THE FUTURE ROLE OF SCHOOL BOARDS

The rapidly changing polities of education and continuing national saliency of school issues will provide new leadership opportunities for school boards. As bodies of lay elected officials at the nexus between school-based and state reform initiatives, they will be uniquely positioned to build coalitions with new influential participants in educational decision making such as business leaders, to broker the necessary communications between school building and state-level policymakers on issues such as finance and "restructuring," to coordinate programs more closely with related human service agencies, and to spearhead efforts to provide education with the broader political base it will so badly need in the challenging years ahead. Indeed, school board members in their self-assessment responses in the IEL project acknowledged their need to build stronger relationships with general government and other children and family service agencies.

The critically important erosion of education's political base of support, which we alluded to earlier, poses new challenges and possible new roles for school boards. Under the assumption that state and local elected officials likely will respond to the money and influence of older voters, it may well be necessary for school boards to devote more attention to building new coalitions with business leaders, senior citizens, and other groups. The growing interest in education being manifested by the business community should be welcomed by school boards. The private sector has begun to recognize that the nation's economic survival in an increasingly competitive international economy will depend on the capacity òf the schools to produce a capable workforce. Business leaders are also recognizing that investments in education are not just philanthropy but manifestations of enlightened self-interest. The inextricable link between education and the economy is the handle through which business and other politically essential support can be mustered to assist the schools. School boards should be more proactive and less passive in the creation of new, more broadly gauged coalitions to support public education.

There are a whole host of education reform issues that need to be addressed, not the least of which is the essential support and commitment that must be forthcoming from school boards if increasing efforts to "restructure" schools by delegating key budget and personnel decisions to the building level are to succeed. At a time when many states are facing severe fiscal constraints, serious questions arise as to whether or not the states will be able to fund reform and school improvement initiatives. The states have never made substantial investments in research, planning, and evaluation (even today over half the support for state agency staff is provided by federal dollars), and the current fiscal prognosis hardly augurs well for new dollars being available to buttress these functions in state education agencies. Indeed, there has been growing tension between wealthy and influential suburban-type districts and state departments as the latter have assumed greater responsibility in monitoring the reform initiatives of recent years. These wealthy districts in many cases have the resources to pay much higher salaries than state government can afford for specialized staff in the research, planning, and evaluation areas. Such staff in local districts understandably resent the encroachments of state officials who are less well trained and less prepared to provide leadership in such substantive areas.

There has been the danger in more than a few states of open conflict breaking out between these influential and relatively independent "lighthouse" districts and the state education agencies that have been given new authority and responsibilities to regulate school systems. State agencies have had to be politically sophisticated in differentiating how they treat diverse districts. In a number of cases, states have been compelled to retreat as a result of charges that they were curbing the creativity of "superior," relatively well-financed, and politically well-connected districts in the states' efforts to improve the bottom rung of school systems.

School boards are obviously centrally involved in such local-state issues and should more proactively seek to broker diverse points of view and perspectives on the educational policymaking prerogatives and capacities of the several levels of government. The last thing that public education needs is overt dysfunctional "no-win" conflicts between state and local officials.

School boards could provide new forms of leadership. Indeed, to cite the words of the famous philosopher Pogo, "they are beleaguered by insurmountable opportunities." Those involved in public education can no longer engage in the internecine warfare that has historically characterized relationships in education—for example, the teachers fight the school boards, public institutions battle their private school counterparts, and elementary-secondary education openly competes with higher education for financing. In other words, school people can no longer pull the wagons around in a circle and shoot inwardly.

School board members as lay people with important policymaking responsibilities and without the inherent conflicts of interest of professional educators are well positioned to serve as credible and necessary brokers between the schools and the outside world. They commonly have political clout and grass roots legitimacy due to their elected status and base in communities.

However, if school boards are to capitalize on their legitimacy and status and propel themselves into a leading role for education reform, boards will have to examine their priorities and their performance as governing bodies.

Citizens, education reformers, and politicians are demanding accountability from the public schools, in fact, much of the states' reform agendas reflect the perception that school boards and education professionals were and are paying too little attention to student outcomes. School boards can change this perception through strengthening demands in their policies for accountability from the system they govern and by exercising strong oversight of their policies. Boards can demonstrate in how they spend their time that outcomes for students are their priority. This requires that school boards focus greater energy and time on goal setting and planning, and that they establish objectives for the school district and cause, through their policies, each school to develop goals and objectives. Boards will need to exercise greater leadership to assure that there are indicators of progress toward objectives and that these measures for accountability are understood by citizens as well as by school district staff.

If they are to reach their own objective for being proactive rather than reactive players in education reform, school boards (individually and collectively through their state associations) will have to shift priorities and spend less time on the day-to-day happenings in their school districts and focus more of their attention on providing leadership for the major policy issues in education. From both IEL's 1986 study findings and our board self-assessment data, it is clear that boards spend too little time discussing major education issues within their own ranks and with their communities. If boards are not on top of the major policy issues and relating these to their own districts, changing from reactive to proactive players will continue to be an elusive goal for them. School boards should become leaders in efforts to promote and implement educational change and improvement— not just because they want to be perceived as being proactive, but because their grass roots governing role is pivotal to substantive and lasting school reform. Boards will be "done unto" and resist, or they will "do" and make reform happen.

An additional area identified in the IEL project in which school boards will have to become more effective to gain credibility for an enhanced leadership role is their policies and practices for parent and community involvement with the schools. While not every school district, or even every urban district, will establish citizen governance of individual schools such as now is in place in Chicago, the trend to involve parents and others in planning and having a real say about what happens in individual schools is growing. School boards need to confront this emerging reality and take a proactive anticipatory stance in their policies. Data from the boards in the IEL sample indicate that few boards believe they have effective policies for meaningfully involving parents and other citizens with their school districts, or for involving them in planning and goal setting in individual schools. Boards that are proactive in these issues will gain respect for their openness in sharing control, and will gain informed partners with which to share responsibility for the schools.

School boards can provide important leadership for education if they will step out of their all too common pattern of reflecting the status quo or their "mirror-like" representation of board members' often conflicting constituencies. As elected or politically appointed lay leaders, they can broker and spearhead efforts to develop a much broader political base for public education in the challenging years ahead by building bridges to general government, the business community, senior citizens, human service agencies, and other noneducation constituencies. With the demographic changes both eroding the political clout of public education and increasing the number of students with complex needs to meet if they are to be successfully educated, schools must expand their base of support. School boards can and should be major catalysts in leading these important efforts.

And finally, school boards must begin to exhibit some risk-taking leadership in their school districts and as the collective school board community. They need to educate complacent citizens to the fact that the schools that worked for them are simply not going to meet the educational needs of today's and tomorrow's students. Citizens need to hear that the continued social, economic, and civic viability of their communities depends on the products of the schools. In the school districts that are demonstrably failing to educate students, school boards need to play "hard ball" politics for all children and youth, not for the self-interests of school board members or clamorous special constituencies. For school boards to become effective leaders in education, they will have to demonstrate in the behavior of their members that conflicting points of view and differing primary loyalties can be reconciled, because the future of children is at stake.

REFERENCE

Institute for Educational Leadership. *School Boards: Strengthening Grassroots Leadership.* Washington, D.C.: IEL Publications Department, 1986.

CHAPTER 7

A Profile of School Board Presidents

C. Emily Feistritzer

School boards are the local governing bodies in America's public educational system. The 40 million students enrolled in approximately 84,000 public elementary and secondary schools are under the jurisdiction of more than 15,000 school districts across the nation. Each school district is governed by a school board and administered by a superintendent.

Between November 15, 1988, and February 10, 1989, the National Center for Education Information (NCEI) conducted a survey of school board presidents to determine who these individuals are and what they think about a wide variety of issues concerning education in America. NCEI conducted a similar survey of school superintendents and public and private school principals in fall 1987. Many of the questions asked in both surveys had also been asked of the general public and of parents of public school students in surveys conducted by other polling groups, such as the Gallup organization.

This chapter contains excerpts from *Profile of School Board Presidents in the U.S.* (Feistritzer, 1989), which analyzes the results of questionnaires completed by 1,217 presidents (or chairs) of school boards throughout the United States. It also compares the responses of school board presidents with those of superintendents, public school principals, the general public, and parents of public school students on a number of critical issues facing education in this nation. The data are also analyzed across several subgroups, including size of school districts, metropolitan status of communities, age groups, sex, political views, degrees held, and years of service as a school board member.

These analyses are of critical importance in getting a true picture of what is going on in America's education system. The tremendous range in size of school districts and the communities in which schools are located are variables that cannot be overlooked.

The distribution of school districts by enrollment size of district, along with the most recent data on number of districts by enrollment size from the U.S. Department of Education, is shown in Table 7.1. It should be noted that three-fourths of the school districts enroll fewer than 2,500 students each and account for fewer than a fourth of all the students enrolled in public schools. On the other hand, 635 school districts (about 4 percent) enroll 10,000 or more students each and collectively account for 45 percent of total school enrollment. One percent of all the school districts enroll more than a quarter of all students. Further, 16 school districts in this country enroll 100,000 or more students each, and together they enroll about 8 percent of all the students.

At the other end of the scale, 4,041 school districts—more than a fourth of all districts—enroll fewer than 300 students each and account for 1.3 percent of total public elementary and secondary student enrollment in this country.

These facts are very important in such considerations as whether or not a school board president favors local school autonomy. The probability that there is only one school in the smaller school districts is about 100 percent. Local school autonomy is a moot issue in these districts.

It is important to put the number and size of school districts in the context of the structure of the United States by metropolitan areas. A census is conducted every decade in the United States. The last census was in 1980. That census showed there were 22,529 "incorporated places" in the United States, 13,706 of which (61 percent) were classified as rural. Census data indicated that 26 percent of the population lived in rural areas of the country.

The breakdown of the overall population by types of communities

Table 7.1
Public School Districts and Enrollment, by Size of District
1987–88

| Enrollment Size | School Districts | | Enrollment |
of District	Number	Percentage	Percentage
Total	15,577	100.0	100.0*
25,000+	171	1.1	27.3
10,000–24,999	464	3.0	17.4
7,500–9,999	330	2.1	7.2
5,000–7,499	607	4.0	9.3
2,500–4,999	1,912	12.3	16.8
2,000–2,499	841	5.4	4.8
1,500–1,999	1,123	7.2	4.9
1,000–1,499	1,597	10.2	5.0
800–999	781	5.0	1.8
600–799	1,015	6.5	1.8
450–599	1,012	6.5	1.3
300–449	1,278	8.2	1.2
150–299	1,686	10.8	0.9
1–149	2,355	15.1	0.4
Size not reported	405	2.6	0.0

* Percentage totals may not add to 100 because of rounding.

will not be updated until the 1990 census.* However, the number of "places," as of July 1, 1986, was 19,101. Of these places, 24 are urban areas with populations of 500,000 or more, and 84 are urban areas having populations between 150,000 and 499,999.

All these population statistics are important in light of the school district arrangement we have in this country and in terms of NCEI's survey of school board presidents.

We sent questionnaires to the school board presidents in 2,197 school districts. Of the 1,217 responses we received, 21 were from school board presidents who identified their communities as being in an inner city with 500,000 or more residents and 52 were from school board presidents in communities with populations between 150,000 and 499,999. While the sample sizes appear small for these subcategories of school board presidents, we surveyed just about all the presidents of large inner-city school boards.

* Summary data for the 1990 census are not yet available.

School board presidents who represented districts having 10,000 or more students were oversampled in this survey in order to achieve enough respondents to allow independent analysis of this crucial segment that represents approximately 45 percent of all students enrolled in public elementary and secondary schools in this country. For purposes of analyzing the responses of all school board presidents throughout the country, each of these segments by district enrollment size (fewer than 2,500; 2,500–9,999; and 10,000 or more) were weighted to their proper proportion of all U.S. school board presidents.

This study provides much new information about the people chairing our school boards. The full report includes thirty-eight tables giving information about who these presidents are and what they think, how they compare with school administrators, how their attitudes on a variety of issues compare with those of the general public, and what we might expect in the future.

DEMOGRAPHIC PROFILE

Presidents of school boards look like school board members generally, and amazingly like the superintendents who work for them. They are overwhelmingly white, predominantly male, in their late forties, married, and have children at home. They have more education, have higher incomes, and are politically more conservative than the average American.

Sex

Women are more represented in the ranks of school board presidents than they are in superintendencies. Nearly three out of ten (29 percent) of school board presidents are women, while only 4 percent of superintendents are women. Thirty-nine percent of school board members are women, according to a survey conducted by the National School Boards Association (Cameron, Underwood, and Fortune, 1988).

There are more women presidents of school boards in large districts than in small ones. While women compose 27 percent of school board presidents in districts that enroll 2,500 or fewer students, they make up 35 percent of those in districts enrolling 10,000 or more students and 32 percent in districts enrolling between 2,500 and 9,999 students. The largest representation of women school board presidents occurs in suburban areas and medium-sized inner cities (36 percent each), and the smallest in rural communities (25 percent).

Race

School board presidents are disproportionately white, as are school superintendents, and school board members generally. An overwhelming 97 percent of presidents are white, 2 percent are black, 1 percent are Hispanic, and fewer than 1 percent are "other races." This compares with 97 percent of superintendents, and 94 percent of all school board members, who are white. Eighty-five percent of the U.S. population today is white. Of all employed persons in the United States, 87 percent are white. Whites represent 92 percent of those in the category of "executives, administrators, and managers," and 90 percent in "professional specialties." Blacks make up 12 percent of the total population, 10 percent of all employed persons, 5 percent of executives, administrators, and managers, 7 percent of workers in professional specialties, and 6 percent of all college graduates in the workforce.

In the administrative ranks of public elementary and secondary schools, blacks make up 1 percent of superintendents, 6 percent of principals, and 6 percent of teachers. One percent of principals and 2 percent of teachers in private schools are black.

Whites make up 76 percent of all students enrolled in public elementary and secondary schools, and 90 percent of all students in private schools. Black students account for 16 percent of all students in public schools, and 6 percent in private schools. The racial composition of school district enrollments varies considerably across the United States. While public school enrollment, overall, is 24 percent minority, and rising nationally, the differences by type of community are striking. Slightly more than a fourth of students enrolled in elementary and secondary schools are enrolled in inner cities (26 percent), but 54 percent of all black students, and 52 percent of Hispanic students, are enrolled in inner-city schools.

According to the 1980 census, 32 percent of all U.S. inhabitants lived in inner cities. The distribution by race was as follows: whites, 27 percent; blacks, 60 percent; persons of Spanish origin, 53 percent; American Indians, 22 percent; Asians and Pacific Islanders, 48 percent; and "other races," 57 percent. In this context, it should be noted that 69 percent of school districts in the United States are in communities identified as rural, compared with only 9 percent in urban areas and 32 percent in suburbs.

Highest Level of Education

While three out of ten (30 percent) of school board presidents have a degree beyond a bachelor's, four out of ten (41 percent) have less than a bachelor's degree. The variation in these data by size of school district is striking. While 17 percent of school board presidents in large school districts have a law, medical, or doctorate degree, 7 percent of those in communities that enroll 2,500 or fewer students have any one of these degrees. Nearly a fourth (24 percent) of presidents in large districts have a master's or other postbaccalaureate degree, compared with 15 percent of those in the smaller districts.

More than half (55 percent) of school board presidents in districts that enroll 2,500 or fewer students have one, two, or three years of college (25 percent), a high school diploma (19 percent), or less than twelve years of schooling (1 percent) as their highest level of education. In the largest school districts, 6 percent of the school board presidents have a high school diploma as their highest level of education, and 24 percent have one, two, or three years of college. Of Americans twenty-five years or older, one in five (19.6 percent) has at least a bachelor's degree.

Occupation

About a third of school board presidents identify the kind of work they do as "managers/administrators, not school administrators" (32 percent). A third (31 percent) also say they work in "professional occupations." Nearly a fifth (17 percent) say they work in small business/sales and 13 percent say they work as "teacher/professor." Nearly a fifth (18 percent) report their work is in farming/agriculture, 10 percent say they work as a "technical/skilled worker," 5 percent as a "clerical" worker, and 2 percent as an "unskilled, semi-skilled worker."

The variation in occupations of school board presidents is most notable in the smallest districts and in different types of communities. A fourth of the presidents in rural communities and 22 percent in districts that enroll fewer than 2,500 students are in agricultural occupations, compared with 2 percent in districts that enroll 10,000 or more students and none in the largest urban areas. The highest concentration of school board presidents who are "managers/administrators" are in districts that enroll 10,000 or more students and those that enroll between 2,500 and 9,999 students (40 percent each). This compares with 29 percent of school board presidents in districts that enroll fewer than 2,500 students who are in managerial or administrative occupations. Forty-one percent of school board presidents in suburban areas and 44 percent in cities with populations between 150,000 and 499,999 are in management or administrative jobs. This is compared with 28 percent in rural areas, 32 percent in smaller urban areas, and 25 percent in the largest inner cities.

Marital Status

School officials tend to represent the traditional family considerably more than does the overall population. While 57 percent of all households in this country are married-couple households, 94 percent of school board presidents as well as 94 percent of superintendents and 87 percent of public school principals are married. Only 3 percent of school board presidents, 4 percent of superintendents, and 7 percent of principals in public schools are divorced or separated. Half of married school board presidents report that their spouses are employed full time, 22 percent say their spouses work part time, and 27 percent said their spouses were unemployed.

Nearly two-thirds (64 percent) of school-board-president households have children under eighteen in them. This compares with only 35 percent of all American households and 47 percent of all married-couple households that have children under eighteen living in them.

Nearly seven out of ten (68 percent) school-board-president households in school districts enrolling fewer than 2,500 students have children under eighteen in them, compared with 51 percent of those in the largest districts and 55 percent in those districts that enroll between 2,500 and 9,999 students. In rural areas, 69 percent of school-board-president households have children in them, compared with 55 percent in inner cities with populations of 500,000 or more, 51 percent in cities between 150,000 and 499,999, 52 percent in other urban areas, and 56 percent in suburban areas.

Salary and Household Income

The range of annual earnings reported by school board presidents is quite wide. While 13 percent report annual earnings of $75,000 or more, 20 percent say they earn less than $25,000 per year, and an additional 19 percent report earnings between $25,000 and $35,000. The median annual earnings falls in the $40,000–$44,999 range. A third (33 percent) of the school board presidents report annual earnings of $50,000 or more. This compares with 51 percent of school superintendents, 21 percent of all college graduates working full time, year round, and 4.8 percent of all workers in America who earn $50,000 or more per year. Thirteen percent of school board presidents, 7 percent of superintendents, 8.2 percent of college graduates working full time, and 1.6 percent of all workers earn $75,000 or more a year.

SCHOOL BOARD MATTERS

Length of School Board Service

All school board presidents have been members of their school boards, a high proportion of them for several years. More than a fourth (26 percent) of all school board presidents have been a member of their current school board fourteen or more years. Nine percent have been school board members for fifteen or more years. Although their proportions are small, there are some presidents who have served on their school board for twenty-five years or more (1.1 percent overall, and 1.5 percent among presidents in the smallest districts with enrollments under 2,500).

Male school board presidents tend to have served as members longer than women. Twelve percent of male presidents, compared with 2 percent of female presidents, have been members of their school board for fifteen years or more. Those with the least education also have served longest. Twelve percent of presidents who have less than a bachelor's degree—compared with 6 percent who have a J.D., M.D., or Ph.D., 8 percent who have a master's or other postbaccalaureate degree, and 7 percent whose highest level of education is a bachelor's degree—have been members of their school board fifteen years or more.

Children in School

Most of the nation's school board presidents have children of their own enrolled in either elementary or secondary schools and/or in colleges or universities. In addition, most of these children attend public rather than private educational institutions.

Nearly two thirds (64 percent) of school board presidents have children currently enrolled in public elementary or secondary schools in their own districts. Seven percent report having children enrolled in public elementary or secondary schools in a district other than where they are president, 1 percent have children in a religiously affiliated private elementary or secondary school, and fewer than 1 percent have children enrolled in nonreligious private schools. More presidents in small districts tend to have children enrolled in elementary or secondary schools in their districts than do those in other districts. Board presidents in rural communities represent the largest proportion who have their own children enrolled in their district (68 percent). Only 31 percent of school board presidents in cities with populations of a half million or more have children enrolled in their own district. Virtually none of the school board presidents, in any size district or community, send their children to nonreligious private schools. However, four out of the twenty-one respondents in cities of more than 500,000 population report having children enrolled in religiously affiliated private elementary and secondary schools.

A significant proportion of presidents said they have children enrolled in colleges and universities—more in public (30 percent) than in private (10 percent) institutions. The practice of school board presidents sending their own children to private colleges or universities is most common among those who reside in communities with over 150,000 population or in suburbs, as well as those who head school boards which enroll more than 2,500 students.

Jobs in Education

Most school board presidents have never held a job in education, either as a classroom teacher or as an administrator. Sixty-eight percent of presidents said they have never worked in the educational system in any capacity. This was most prevalent among those in small school districts with enrollments of less than 2,500 (70 percent) and those who reside in rural communities (73 percent). Of those who said they had worked in education, most had been classroom teachers in elementary or secondary schools. One in five (20 percent) school board presidents had been an elementary or secondary school teacher. The second largest group of presidents with prior educational experience said they had worked as college or university professors (8 percent). School board presidents who said they had been in educational jobs were in roles other than teaching or administration (7 percent), had been college or university administrators (3 percent), or had served as elementary or secondary school principals (3 percent). Fewer than 1 percent had previously worked as school superintendents. Nine percent of school board presidents said they were holding a job in education when they were elected to the school board. Of these, 30 percent were elementary or secondary teachers, 39 percent were college professors, 3 percent were elementary or secondary school principals, 12 percent were college administrators, and 16 percent reported having held some other job in education.

Hours per Week Spent on School Board Activities

Nine out of ten school board presidents report spending fewer than fifteen hours per week on school board activities (89 percent), with the largest proportions reporting that they spend one to two hours (18 percent), three to four hours (25 percent), or five to six hours (22 percent) each week on school board business. Hardly any presidents report spending more than twenty-five hours per week on school board activities. The reported work habits did not vary greatly, regardless of whether presidents had previous educational work experience either as teachers or administrators at the elementary, secondary, or college level. Those who had no previous educational experience were more likely than the others to spend fewer than nine hours each week on school board business. The responses indicated that the longer a president has served on a school board, the less time he or she devoted each week to school board activities.

Women who are school board presidents devote more time to school board activities than do their male counterparts. While 57 percent of female presidents said they spend seven or more hours per week on school board work, 75 percent of the male presidents said they spend fewer than seven hours each week on school board business. Half of the male presidents, compared with a fourth of the female presidents, report spending fewer than five hours per week on school board activities.

School board presidents in the largest districts, with enrollments over 10,000 students, spend considerably more time each week on school board activities than do presidents in smaller districts. Three-fourths (78 percent) of presidents in districts enrolling fewer than 2,500 students spend fewer than seven hours per week on school board activities. This compares with 85 percent of presidents in districts that enroll 10,000 students and over, who spend more than seven hours per week. The median number of hours spent on school board activities by presidents in the largest districts is twelve hours, in medium districts, seven hours, and in small districts, five hours.

Perceptions of Time Spent on School Board Activities

School board presidents were asked about the amounts of time they spend on various tasks in the course of their school board work, and whether these were "the right amounts, too much, or too little." They said they spend "too much time" in matters related to labor relations—negotiating/bargaining with teacher groups (30 percent) and bargaining with groups that represent employees other than teachers (12 percent). They felt they spend "too little time" on interacting with other local governing bodies (48 percent); selecting/adopting school curricula (45 percent); selecting/adopting textbooks (37 percent); meeting/conferring with teacher groups and discussing changing demographics of the student population, such as "children at risk" (both 36 percent); and student test scores/achievement measures and ceremonial/ritualistic/awards/ recognition activities (both 30 percent). There was considerable agreement on those tasks on which the majority of school board presidents felt they spent "the right amount of time," all of which dealt with discipline: due process hearings for students (86 percent); student disciplinary action (85 percent); making personnel decisions (84 percent); and due process hearings for personnel (83 percent). By and large, school board presidents are satisfied with the amount of time they are spending on a wide range of school board activities. On only two out of eighteen suggested activities ("interacting with other local governing bodies" and "national/state educational issues") did fewer than half of the school board presidents report they were not spending the right amount of time.

Decision-making Authority

The school board presidents were asked to specify which participants in the educational process "currently have" the ultimate
decision-making responsibility in various school-related matters in
their districts, and which "should have" this power. The responses to
these items seem to indicate that school board presidents are fairly
satisfied with the status quo when it comes to who makes decisions.

In each category, the respondents gave the lowest ratings to parents in having the ultimate responsibility for decisions on a range of
educational matters. Only 10 percent of the presidents felt that parents currently have the ultimate decision-making responsibility in
selecting curricula, while 14 percent said parents should have this
responsibility. Regarding parent responsibility for principal evaluation, 11 percent said parents currently do have this responsibility,
while 12 percent said parents should have it. Eleven percent said
parents should have responsibility for decisions on extracurricular
activities and for what curriculum materials are used. Ten percent
said parents should have responsibility in selecting textbooks, and 9
percent said parents should have responsibility in deciding academic
standards and for approving line items in the budget of the district.

About half of the school board presidents said that teachers currently
do and should have primary responsibility for selecting textbooks, choosing methodology/pedagogy, and deciding what curriculum materials are
used. They also rated school board and superintendent responsibility in
selecting curriculum relatively high.

While 44 percent said the ultimate responsibility for selecting
teachers rests, and 40 percent said it should rest, with superintendents, there was an indication of some support for principals having
more authority in this area. Principals were judged to have the
greatest responsibility for teacher evaluation (70 percent said that
principals currently have this responsibility, and 67 percent believed
that they should have it). However, the responses showed that a small
percentage of school board presidents feel this responsibility should
be reduced for principals and increased for school boards and
superintendents.

The presidents believed that the greatest current responsibilities for
superintendents were for principal evaluation (74 percent) and for
line items within the district budget (53 percent). Slightly fewer
presidents felt the superintendents should have these responsibilities
(71 and 49 percent).

The school board presidents believed that school boards have and should continue to have primary responsibility for overall school district budget (73 and 76 percent, respectively), dismissal of teachers (56 and 57 percent, respectively), dismissal of principals (64 and 64 percent, respectively), selection of principals (58 and 56 percent, respectively), and disciplinary policies (61 and 57 percent, respectively).

Influence of Various Groups on the School Board

If what the presidents of school boards surveyed say about who influences school board decision making, and to what degree, is accurate, school boards are indeed fairly autonomous governing bodies. With the exception of the superintendent and district central office, the state department of education, and to a lesser extent, the federal department of education, no group was felt to exert much influence on the decision making of school boards. Parents and parent groups are perceived to have the least influence.

It comes as no surprise that virtually all (99 percent) of the school board presidents said the superintendent in their district influenced the decision making of their board. Eighty-one percent said the superintendent had "great influence" on decision making. Second in order of influence was the state department of education. Nearly nine out of ten presidents surveyed (88 percent) said the state department of education had either "great" (51 percent) or "some" (37 percent) influence. A fourth (24 percent) reported the U.S. Department of Education had "great influence." Yet 30 percent said the federal department of education did not have much influence over their decision making (24 percent) or had no influence at all (6 percent).

Teacher unions and professional organizations were perceived to have a "great influence" by 14 percent of the school board presidents, "some influence" by 49 percent, "not much influence" by 26 percent, and "no influence at all" by 10 percent. Those identified as having the least influence on the decision making of the school board were individual parents, the Parent-Teachers Association, and "special interest groups."

Federal Government Influence on Local Schools

School board presidents, as well as superintendents and principals, are at odds with the general public on whether or not the federal government should have more or less influence on improving local public schools. The public favors more. All school officials want less. When asked, "Would you like the federal government in Washington to have more influence, less influence, or about the same amount of influence?" 37 percent of the adults polled by the Gallup organization in the spring of 1987 said the federal government should have more influence, and 39 percent said it should have less. When NCEI surveyed school board presidents in the winter of 1988–89, only 7 percent of them said the federal government should have more influence in improving schools. When surveyed by NCEI in the fall of 1987, 9 percent of the superintendents and 10 percent of public school principals said the federal government should have more influence.

ATTITUDES ABOUT PUBLIC SCHOOLS

The general public does not give the schools very high marks, either in the nation as a whole or in their own communities. The presidents of school boards make a clear distinction between what they think about schools in the nation as a whole and what they think about the schools in their own jurisdictions. They are much more in agreement with the general public about schools as a whole, and much more in alignment with school administrators concerning the schools in their own communities. When asked, "Do you think the educational standards in our schools have improved in recent years, stayed the same, or become worse?" 29 percent of the presidents said schools had "become worse," and 43 percent said schools had improved. When polled in a TIME/Yankelovich Clancy Schulman survey in February 1987, 49 percent of adults responded "become worse," and 41 percent said standards had improved. When NCEI asked the same question in its survey of superintendents and principals in the fall of 1987, 81 percent of the superintendents and 72 percent of public school principals said standards in our schools had improved. However, when school board presidents were asked, "Would you say that the public schools in your community have improved from, say, five years ago, gotten worse, or stayed about the same?" 74 percent said the schools in their own communities had improved, and only 5 percent said they had gotten worse.

The general public was asked this question by the Gallup organization in spring 1988 (Gallup and Elam, 1988). At that time, 29 percent said schools in their own communities had improved, and 19 percent said they had gotten worse. Thirty-nine percent of the parents of public school students responded that schools had improved, compared with 16 percent who said they had gotten worse. Only 25 percent of adults who had no children in school said that schools in their communities had improved in the last five years. This is significant because two-thirds of households in the United States today do not have children under eighteen years of age living in them.

When superintendents and principals were asked by NCEI in fall 1987 if the schools in their own communities had improved, gotten worse, or stayed about the same in the last five years, 87 percent of the superintendents and 75 percent of the principals said they had improved.

U.S. Schools and Schools in Other Countries

When presidents of school boards were asked how public education in the United States compares with school systems in other countries, they were much more in line with what the general public thinks than they were with what the school administrators think. When asked if the U.S. system of public education is strong or weak in comparison with those in Japan, Great Britain, West Germany, and other major western countries, 55 percent of school board presidents and 48 percent of the public think the U.S. system is strong. Eighty-five percent of superintendents and 67 percent of public school principals also think the U.S. system of public education is strong in comparison with other countries.

Grading the Schools

The split between how school board presidents rate public schools nationally and those in their own communities holds up in the grades they give schools. Only 2 percent of the presidents give public schools nationally an A, yet 23 percent of them give the schools in their own communities an A. An additional 56 percent give the schools in their own communities a B. Fewer than a third (31 percent) of school board presidents give schools nationally a B.

Only 3 percent of the adults surveyed by the Gallup organization in April 1988 gave schools nationally an A, and only 9 percent gave the schools in their own communities an A. Five percent of superintendents surveyed in the fall of 1987 by NCEI gave schools nationally an A, and 32 percent gave the schools in their communities the highest grade. An additional 66 percent of superintendents assigned a grade of B to schools nationally, and 58 percent gave B's to their own schools.

Presidents of school boards in the larger school districts think more positively about schools in the nation as a whole than do those in the smaller districts. Fifty-six percent of the presidents in districts that enroll 10,000 or more students, compared with 42 percent in those enrolling fewer than 2,500 students, think educational standards have improved in recent years. When grading schools in their own communities, school board presidents in suburban and smaller urban areas give higher marks than do presidents in other types of communities. Grades of A or B were given to schools in their own communities by 86 percent of presidents in suburban communities, by 82 percent in small urban areas, by 78 percent in rural areas, by 67 percent in cities between 150,000 and 499,999, and by 60 percent in cities with populations of 500,000 or more.

ATTITUDES ABOUT WAYS TO IMPROVE THE U.S. EDUCATIONAL SYSTEM

Among the proposals advanced in recent years to improve the educational system in the United States are the following:

1. Restructuring to allow greater autonomy at the local level, more decision-making authority at the school building level, teacher "empowerment" (giving teachers greater authority in the running of schools), and involving parents and students more directly in the running of schools.
2. Recruiting educated adults who have experience in careers other than education to be teachers and administrators.
3. Making the school year and school day longer.
4. Demanding more accountability from students, as well as from schools.

NCEI asked school board presidents whether they strongly agreed, somewhat agreed, somewhat disagreed, or strongly disagreed with ten separate reform proposals. Some results of this survey are summarized here.

More Autonomy at the Building Level and Teacher Empowerment

Allowing individual schools to determine how they will operate was favored by nearly two-thirds of all school board presidents. However, only one-third said they agreed that "giving the teachers greater authority in the running of schools" would improve the U.S. educational system. The reform proposals with the greatest differences among subcategories of school board presidents were school building autonomy and teacher empowerment.

While 68 percent of school board presidents in districts that enroll fewer than 2,500 students favor "letting each individual school decide how the school will operate," only 45 percent of those in the districts that enroll 10,000 or more students and 48 percent of those in districts that enroll between 2,500 and 9,999 agree with the statement.

It should be remembered that three-fourths of the school board presidents in the United States are in districts that enroll fewer than 2,500 students, and a large proportion of these are in districts that have only one or two schools in the entire district. The districts that enroll 10,000 or more students account for fewer than 5 percent of all the school districts in the nation. Yet they enroll nearly half of all students enrolled in public elementary and secondary schools. The school board presidents in these largest school districts, while not as much in favor of letting individual schools decide how they will run, are more in favor of giving teachers greater authority in the running of schools. Slightly more than half (54 percent) of presidents of school boards in districts that enroll 10,000 or more students said they agreed that giving teachers greater authority in the running of schools would improve the U.S. educational system. Thirty-one percent of presidents in districts enrolling fewer than 2,500 students and 40 percent of those in districts that enroll between 2,500 and 9,999 students also agreed on giving greater authority to teachers.

Noticeable differences on these proposals also exist among school board presidents by metropolitan status of their communities. While only 27 percent of the presidents in rural communities (where about a fourth of all students are enrolled) agreed with empowering teachers,

70 percent of those in inner cities with populations of 500,000 or more (where another fourth of the students are enrolled) agreed with the proposal. About half of the presidents in the other types of communities favor giving teachers more authority in the running of schools—47 percent in inner cities with populations between 150,000 and 499,999, 51 percent in other urban areas, and 41 percent in suburban communities.

There is a similar split on the proposal to have each individual school decide how it will operate. Seventy percent of presidents in the largest inner cities and 68 percent of those in rural areas favor this proposal. Again, about half of those presidents in other types of communities are in favor—43 percent of those in inner cities with populations between 150,000 and 499,999, 53 percent in other urban areas, and 54 percent in suburban areas.

Presidents who have never held any job in education are more favorable to local school autonomy and less favorable to teacher empowerment than those who have held jobs in education. Two-thirds (66 percent) of school board presidents who have never held any job in education favor local school autonomy, compared with 54 percent who have held a job as a teacher or administrator in elementary schools and 47 percent who have held a job as a professor or administrator in a college or university.

Conservative school board presidents favor local school autonomy most and teacher empowerment least. Two-thirds (66 percent) of school board presidents who say they are "conservative" agree that letting each individual school decide how it will operate would improve our educational system, but only 28 percent of them think giving teachers greater authority in running schools would have that effect. On the other end of the political spectrum, 57 percent of school board presidents who identify themselves as "liberal" agree with teacher empowerment, and 56 percent agree with individual school autonomy.

Involving Parents in Running the Schools

About two-thirds of the school board presidents across all groups agreed that involving parents more directly in the running of schools would improve our educational system. The strongest support came from those in the largest inner cities and from presidents who are newest to their school boards. Eighty-five percent of presidents in inner cities with populations of 500,000 or more and 73 percent of presidents who had been members of their boards from one to three years agreed with this proposal. Women presidents favor the proposal more than men: 70 percent of the women and 61 percent of the men.

The public and parents of children in school say parents of public school children should have more say regarding the curriculum, that is, the courses offered. Public school authorities, on the other hand, think parents have about the right amount of say concerning the curriculum. While 45 percent of the general public and 51 percent of public school parents said parents should have more say in curricular matters, only 16 percent of school board presidents, 14 percent of superintendents, and 13 percent of public school principals said parents should have more say regarding what courses are offered. More than three-fourths of the school officials said parents have the right amount of say in determining the curriculum. Seventy-nine percent of school board presidents, 80 percent of superintendents, and 76 percent of public school principals think parents have the right amount of say regarding what courses are offered. Thirty-seven percent of the general public and 41 percent of public school parents agree with that view.

Recruiting Adults with Experience in Other Careers into Teaching

"Recruiting adults who have experience in careers other than education into teaching" was the second most commonly agreed upon way to improve the U.S. educational system. It was second only to "Demand that a student perform at grade level before he or she is passed on to the next grade."

Three-fourths of all school board presidents favored bringing people from other careers into teaching. Only 5 percent said they "strongly disagreed" with this proposal, and 5 percent said they were not sure. The proposal was more popular among school board presidents in the larger districts and in all types of urban and suburban communities than it was in districts that enroll 2,500 or fewer students. Eighty-six percent of presidents with a J.D., M.D., or Ph.D, 78 percent with a master's or other postbaccalaureate degree, and 82 percent of those with a bachelor's degree agreed with the proposal. Sixty-seven percent of school board presidents with less than a bachelor's degree said they agreed that recruiting adults with careers outside education would improve the educational system. Eighty-nine percent of the presidents who identified themselves as "liberal" were in favor of the proposal, as were 75 percent of those who said they were "moderate" and 72 percent who said they were "conservative."

Recruiting Adults from Other Careers into School Administration

While strongly favoring recruiting adults from other careers into teaching, school board presidents are less enthusiastic about recruiting managers from other careers into school administration. Fewer than half (48 percent) of the presidents agree that this would improve the educational system in the United States. The strongest support came from presidents who had been members of their school board for from one to three years (53 percent). Only 39 percent of presidents of school boards who had served as board members for ten or more years favored the proposal.

Extending the School Day or Year

About half of the school board presidents (51 percent) agreed that extending the school year would improve the educational system, and 48 percent believed that extending the school day would be desirable for the same reason. Nearly two-thirds of the board presidents in the largest districts favored lengthening the school year (65 percent in districts enrolling 10,000 or more students and 64 percent in districts enrolling between 2,500 and 9,999). Fewer than half of the presidents (47 percent) agreed with this proposal. There was a similar response to the proposal to extend the school day. Sixty-four percent of presidents in the largest districts, 59 percent in the mid-sized ones, and 45 percent in the smallest districts agreed that extending the school day would improve the educational system.

The more education a board president has, the more he or she favors extending the school year and the school day. Two-thirds (66 percent) of presidents with a J.D., M.D., or Ph.D agree with extending the school year. Sixty-one percent of those with a master's or other postbaccalaureate degree, 52 percent who have a bachelor's degree, and 44 percent of those presidents with less than a bachelor's degree also favored the proposal. Fifty-nine percent of women presidents and 49 percent of male presidents favor extending the school year, but the percentages of men and women presidents favoring extending the school day were about even, 48 percent and 50 percent, respectively. Fifty-one percent of the presidents who consider themselves "liberal" agree with extending the school day. Smaller percentages of those who consider themselves "moderate" (55 percent) or "conservative" (45 percent) approved an extended day.

Choice

On no issue in the NCEI survey were there greater differences between the views of the general public and those of all types of school officials, including school board presidents, than those pertaining to "choice," that is, giving parents the power to choose the schools their children will attend.

When the public was asked in spring 1987 by the Gallup organization (Gallup and Clark, 1987) whether "the parents in your community should or should not have the right to choose which local schools their children should attend," 71 percent of the general public said they should. More than 76 percent of parents of public school children agreed. Only 36 percent of school board presidents surveyed in winter 1988–89 said "Yes" to the question of choice, as did 31 percent of superintendents surveyed in fall 1987 by NCEI.

Thirty-seven percent of the presidents in the largest districts, 39 percent of those in the smallest districts, and 29 percent of presidents in districts that enroll between 2,500 and 9,999 students favored parental choice. It is important to keep in mind that a large proportion of the school districts enrolling fewer than 2,500 students have only one school. By metropolitan status of the community, choice is slightly more popular among board presidents in the largest inner cities (53 percent). It is less popular among board presidents in rural communities, where 40 percent endorsed the idea. Choice was least popular among presidents in suburban regions, where 28 percent approved.

Most presidents (57 percent) who have served on the school board ten or more years are opposed to parental choice, as are 51 percent of the presidents who have been board members four to six years. The least opposition to choice among school board presidents comes from those who have been on the school board one to three years, 43 percent of whom oppose choice. Forty-three percent of board presidents holding either a J.D., M.D., or Ph.D. are favorable to choice, as are 39 percent of those with a master's or postbaccalaureate degree, 33 percent who hold a bachelor's degree, and 38 percent of those with less than a bachelor's degree.

Of the presidents who identify themselves as "conservative" on most political matters, 39 percent favor choice, as do 36 percent of those calling themselves "moderate" and 29 percent of those who identify themselves as "liberal."

Vouchers

The voucher system is favored by 44 percent of the general public and 49 percent of parents of public school children, whereas only 16 percent of school board members, 8 percent of superintendents, and 13 percent of public school principals favor vouchers. Thirty-six percent of the general public, 38 percent of parents of children in public schools, and 37 percent of nonpublic school parents believed that vouchers would help the public schools in their own communities (Gallup and Clark, 1987). A smaller percentage of school board presidents (11 percent), of superintendents (12 percent), and of public school principals (11 percent) said that vouchers would help public schools in their communities.

Among school board presidents, 86 percent of those considering themselves liberal were opposed to vouchers. However, opposition to vouchers was very strong in all subgroups of school board presidents. Those groups least opposed to vouchers are those in the largest inner cities and those who consider themselves "conservative" on most political matters. Among school board presidents, opposition to vouchers is inversely correlated with the presidents' level of education and directly correlated with the number of years served on the school board.

The facts and figures presented in this report may cause one to pause in the consideration of the massive restructuring begun through federal initiatives and state mandates. Small schools and small districts may be carrying on "with business as usual" while grand plans are laid elsewhere. The statistics presented in this report remind us of the great diversity in sizes and types of American schools and school districts and that all of them need to be considered if the continuing reform and restructuring efforts are to make a lasting impact.

REFERENCES

Cameron, Beatrice H.; Underwood, Kenneth E.; and Fortune, Jim C. "Politics and Power: How You're Selected and Elected to Lead This Nation's Schools," *American School Board Journal* 175 (January, 1988): 17–21.

Feistritzer, Emily C. *Profile of School Board Presidents in the U.S.* Washington, D.C.: National Center for Education Information, 1989

Gallup, Alec M., and Clark, David L. "The 19th Annual Gallup Poll of the Public's Attitudes toward the Public Schools," *Phi Delta Kappan* 69 (September 1987): 20.

Gallup, Alec M., and Elam, Stanley M. "The 20th Annual Gallup Poll of the Public's Attitudes toward the Public Schools," *Phi Delta Kappan* 70 (September 1988): 42.

Section V
From Guarding to Cheerleading: The Changing Roles of School Boards

CHAPTER 8

The Role of School Boards in the Governance of Education

Louis F. Miron and
Robert K. Wimpelberg

INTRODUCTION

Local school boards have recently come under attack from an array of political, institutional, and educational interests. Indeed, the legitimacy of school boards as policymaking institutions is threatened as state "bankruptcy" laws enable the state to take over an entire school district when the academic performance of the district ranks below par. In Chelsea, Massachusetts, the school district has entered into a "partnership" agreement with a private university to manage the districts' schools, calling into question the traditional governance and policymaking roles of local school boards and reconfiguring the board's supervision of the superintendent. The Illinois legislature, under pressure from community groups in Chicago, redistributed local governance power when it created local school councils.

A wave of litigation filed in state courts has challenged state funding formulas for elementary and secondary education. Where these lawsuits have been successful, the courts have thrown out the finance formulas and ordered the legislatures in those states to include curriculum standards to be achieved with the influx of new funds. On the surface, this action has dire consequences for local school boards as presently conceptualized by academics and citizens alike. However, the question of where, historically and philosophically, boards have obtained their authority and power is often poorly understood in such conceptualizations.

We assert that the role of local school boards in the governance of education depends on the state's historical allocation of funds to local school districts. Specifically, the presence of state funding formulas has created a mechanism whereby the state controls education at the local level. Local school boards, therefore, assume a problematic function in governance generally and in policymaking in particular. It is our contention that this problematic relationship with the state is a direct result of control of public education through financial mechanisms. The question of how local boards respond to court orders mandating funding changes is inextricably tied to the financial relationship local school districts have maintained with the state.

In this chapter, we place in historical and theoretical perspective the traditional roles of local school boards in governing and policymaking for elementary and secondary public education in this country. The chapter is divided into four major sections. In part one, we trace the historical and philosophical evolution of local governance of public schooling. In part two, we review state finance cases in Montana, Kentucky, Texas, and New Jersey. In part three, we theorize about the varieties of policymaking roles local school boards can assume. Finally, in part four, we categorize the range of responses to state court actions that are available to local school boards. With examples drawn from recent teacher strikes in Louisiana, we speculate on how crisis can provide opportunities for school boards to engage meaningfully in the formulation and enactment of educational policy.

THE ORIGINS OF GOVERNANCE

The U.S. Constitution does not mention public education, and while the presumption has been that the Tenth Amendment gave governance of education to the states, individual states historically have varied in their understanding of this responsibility. The evolution of state responsibility for—and hence control over—public elementary and secondary education has been attributed to historical precedent related to financial and economic necessity as much as to legal authority. In this section, we examine the early relationship between the church and state and how each viewed the other's role in public education. The discussion will focus on the demands for universal public education and the underlying question of who would control and manage schooling. The question of the state stepping into that control by bargaining with the electorate and ultimately creating a state finance mechanism will be examined, along with its implications for control of local school districts. While the gaining of state control was accomplished, it was not done overnight, nor without significant conflict. That conflict continues today.

The Notion of "Public"

The preamble to the Constitution of the United States begins with the phrase, "We the people, in order to form a more perfect Union." What is the historical context of "we the people" in relation to the governance of elementary and secondary education? Lawrence Cremin (1970) states that "we the people" meant simply the residents of the colonies. These colonial residents asserted their freedom from British rule in the Declaration of Independence, later acknowledged in the Treaty of Paris, and guaranteed their newfound rights in the Articles of Confederation. It was this latter document that served as a foundation for the language of the Constitution. The Articles of Confederation contains the phrase, "all privileges and immunities of free citizens in the several states," and the federal Constitution provided in similar language that "the citizens of each state shall be entitled to all privileges and immunities of citizens in the several states."

However, in the rhetoric of free citizens and privileges, the status of a large portion of the population was ill-defined. Blacks, Indians, and women were not accorded any of these same protections. Certainly a different status was ascribed to those who were landowners as opposed to those who were not. In fact, the free citizenry spoken of in these documents were landed, white, free, and male. Nor did this new Constitution contain any mention of education. Ellwood Cubberley (1919) states:

A search of the debates of the (Constitutional) Convention reveals that only once was anything relating to education brought before the body . . . . It is not surprising, however, when we consider the time, the men, and the existing conditions, that the founders of our Republic did not deem the subject of public education important enough to warrant consideration in the Convention or inclusion in the document. Education almost everywhere was still a *private* matter, and quite generally under the control of the Church. [P. 52]

The new federalists were aware of the importance of education to the nation. The perceived need for education in the early history of the country may be best illustrated by the push for a national university. Many of the founding fathers, most notably Washington and Madison, were captured by this concept. The thinking then focused on the proposed location in the capital as the center for enlightening public opinion. Although there was widespread agreement on this location, establishment of the university was difficult to bring to fruition. Education was not a constitutional function of the government, and hence the federal government was not empowered to accomplish this task. President Jefferson doubted that Congress had the authority under the Constitution to establish a national university, and in 1806, suggested that Congress would need a constitutional amendment prior to considering the concept of a national university. But Congress did not consider the possibility nor was an amendment ever drafted. The issue of who was to govern education was obviously still in serious contention. For example, John Adams argued that it was the role of churches to "nurture the public discipline required for the operation of a free society." That government should be involved in education was still controversial and what role the states would play was not known.

The Influence of the Church

Until the Revolution, the development of education had been regarded as an affair of the church, as were marriage, baptism, burial of the dead, and administration of the sacraments. After the war, the churches continued their efforts to maintain their schools, but the demand for education grew too rapidly. The churches made an effort to expand schooling but were reluctant to change the manner of educating their students and the emphasis they placed on ecclesiastical understanding. "The result was, that with the coming nationality and the slow but gradual growth of a national consciousness, national

pride, national needs, and the gradual development of national resources in the shape of taxable property . . . combined to make secular
instead of religious schools seem both desirable and possible, to a
constantly increasing number of citizens" (Cubberley, 1919,
pp. 83–84).

What existed was the church school with its orientation to classical
learning and to preparing its students for the ministry or law; the few
state universities that took in individuals from only the classical
schools; and the few pauper schools that sought to make the very poor
more capable of being productive, working members of society. A
concern slowly emerged that education needed to be available to
everyone, that it was a necessity for the young country's growth and
survival. As the nation moved from the postrevolutionary years into
the early 1800s, the middle class or workingmen began to connect to
this general diffusion of knowledge. Rush Welter (1962) writes: "By
contrast, although the workingmen advocated public schools for
clearly instrumental reasons, in other respects, their educational doctrine constituted a stunning departure from republican precedent"
(pp. 56–57).

Education for the Workingman

The linkage between the workingmen and education mirrors a shift
in American economic culture from that of an agrarian society to one
going through industrial transformation. In 1780, 2.7 percent of the
population lived in cities; by the start of the Civil War in 1860, the
percentage had increased to 16.1. By 1900, 32.9 percent of the country's people lived in cities. While immigration was a factor in the
economic growth of American society, only about eight thousand
immigrants a year were coming into the United States at the beginning of this movement in population. Thus, these shifts in population
and in the economy embraced a demographic trend. However, the
question of the role of education in the economic growth of the
country, and its niche in the evolving federalism, remained unsettled.

Gradually, the nation came to accept that education was of vital
importance to our society. The important question became the means
by which a state could create a system of education to suit its needs.
On the federal level, education was not constitutionally mandated,
and the states had let the people do as they pleased. That changed as
state legislatures began to pass educational legislation, whereby the

state became the assertive force by creating state superintendents of education and state boards of education. How was this possible?

Taxation

First, the state had to convince its citizens that taxation was possible without substantial conflict. That conflict was manifested in the battles to generate tax support, to eliminate pauper schools, to make the schools entirely free, to establish state supervision, to eliminate sectarianism, to extend the system upward, and to add the state university to crown the system.

Where did the conflict originate? Cubberley (1919, pp. 122–123) lists fourteen reasons why the state would have difficulty assuming control over education through taxation. State control would be impractical and too visionary as legislation; make education too common; not benefit the masses; tend to break down long-established and desirable social barriers; injure private and parochial schools, in which large sums had been spent and "vested" rights established; instill fear in churches that the state would hurt their progress and welfare; and instill fear in non-English-speaking classes that state schools might supplant instruction in their languages.

State control would also facilitate parents' claim that the State had no right to interfere between a parent and his child in the matter of education; tax those parents without children to be educated; take a man's property in order to educate his child; justify the State in taxing peoples' "benevolence"; tax the industrious to educate the indolent; increase taxes to the extent that no state could meet such a drain on its resources over time; and establish a state school and then a state church.

Obviously, some of these reasons have been left behind in history and some continue today. However, between the pressure exerted by those in government and by workingmen to provide universal schooling, these conflicts were pushed to the background. In retrospect, education for every man seemed predestined, but the issue of who would control it and the mechanism that would accomplish this control comprise the historical questions we need to address to analyze contemporary conflicts in governance.

Taxation was the cornerstone issue. Cubberley (1919) observes that the course of the struggle and the outcomes varied among states, but the progress of the conflict proceeded along these lines:

1. Permission [was] granted to communities so desiring to organize a school taxing district, and to tax for school support the property of those consenting and residing therein.
2. Taxation of all property in the taxing district [was] permitted.
3. State aid [was given] to such districts, at first from the income of permanent endowment funds, and later from the proceeds of a small state appropriation or a state or county tax.
4. Compulsory local taxation [was used] to supplement the state or county grant. [P. 131]

When the question of state aid received center stage, compulsory local taxation for education had been established, and the central battle for the creation of a state school system had been won.

The state therefore financed its entry into the control of local education. Local school boards were then seemingly permanently attached to the umbilical cord of state funding. But this fact did not go unnoticed. Daniel Webster argued before the U.S. Supreme Court:

> Individuals have a right to use their own property for purposes of benevolence, either towards the public or towards other individuals. They have a right to exercise this benevolence in such lawful manner as they may choose, and when the government has induced and excited it, by contracting to give perpetuity to the stipulated manner of exercising it, to rescind this contract, and seize on the property, it is not law, but violence. [Butts and Cremin, 1953, p. 212]

Cubberley (1919) wryly notes: "The acceptance of state aid inevitably meant a small but a gradually increasing state control. The first step was the establishment of some form of state aid; the next was the imposing of conditions necessary to secure this state aid" (p. 157).

While school districts in both rural and city areas began to tax to support their particular efforts, it soon became apparent that they were going to need additional financial support to meet the needs of their respective systems. And it was into this breech that the state moved. An alliance was created whereby the citizens and the local communities agreed to state involvement. But in this alliance, who would control education?

State Control over Public Education

Related to the proposals and counterproposals on public support was the question of who should control the schools. As Robert Butts and Lawrence Cremin (1953) have noted:

When education was a private affair conducted largely under the auspices of churches and religious groups, the question of control was a simple one. Control rested largely in the hands of private individuals and ecclesiastical authorities. Now, however, just as public demands for public support of schools grew out of new life conditions and educational conceptions, so did demands for public control. Generally, such demands were of two sorts; first, demands based on the assumptions that public control should inevitably follow public support; and second, demands based on the assumption that if the public did not control the common school, the sectarian interests would get hold of it and impose their particular political, economic, or religious doctrines on the students. This would obviously force some to withdraw in order to preserve their rights to conscience, and the schools would no longer be "equal and open to all." [P. 204]

The notion of public control following public support was implicit in the majority of proposals for spending public money. The custom of control by town authorities had been firmly established in New England. The question of which mechanism the state would use to assume control over education was controversial. A thorny question concerned the ultimate repository of public control over education. At what level—local, county, or state—would such control materialize? The states felt that the Tenth Amendment automatically reserved that responsibility for the state. This was a reasonable interpretation for the states, but the Tenth Amendment stated that the rights not given in the constitution went to the states *or* to the people. The issue remained as to whether the states or the local communities should establish control over public education. Interestingly enough, it was during this period that the states began to ask the districts to create local "school boards" to supervise the districts' activities on behalf of the state. This met with strong opposition in the beginning, but by the 1850s, such boards were beginning to be commonplace.

Reminiscent of the state "takeover" laws of the late 1980s, proposals for state control advanced the argument that centralization would bring higher standards of education to local communities. Only the state could compel minimum standards and assist poor localities to meet these standards. Proponents of state control stressed the fact that the state delegated much of its power to localities. Opponents of state control argued that public education was the primary responsibility of parents and local communities. If the state assumed this responsibility through legal authority, it would "tread directly upon individual rights and democratic local government" (Butts and Cremin, 1953, pp. 204–205).

From then to now, this argument has not waned. The reality,

however, has been that local school boards have depended on the state for both their legal authority and their financial survival. Once local communities accepted and became accustomed to the infusion of state funds, the state settled all arguments by enforcing the concept that it has the right to supervise the expenditure of its funds. Allen Hubsch (1989) notes that on average, local school districts today receive only 40 percent of their funding from local sources. It is through state funding of local public education that state control has been historically asserted. We turn next to the issue of funding, particularly to state finance formulas presently being challenged in state courts.

THE ADJUDICATION OF STATE CONTROL

Recent decisions by state courts have had the effect of reaffirming state control over public elementary and secondary education. Coalitions of lawyers, citizen groups, and "property poor" school districts have successfully challenged finance formulas in a number of states (Thompson, 1990) to establish accountability at the state level and to reestablish control through revamped funding schemes. In a few instances, notably in Montana, Kentucky, and Texas, this activity has resulted in a court order to scrap the entire educational delivery system. Further, the New Jersey Supreme Court ordered the legislature to earmark special funding for at-risk students with special needs. In this section, we provide an overview of the most important of these cases with an eye to analyzing, in the subsequent sections, possible local school board responses to these sweeping decisions.

The Montana Case

Funding for elementary and secondary education in Montana, as in a number of states throughout the country, was dependent on the wealth of a school district. In *Helena Elementary School District No. 1 v. The State of Montana* (1990), plaintiffs successfully argued that the Montana plan for financing public schools violated the state constitutional guarantees to provide an equal public education to all its citizens. The state supreme court ruled that the system of financing public schools was unconstitutional under the state constitution. The court concluded that the distribution of state funds did not mitigate the "great differences in wealth of the various school districts and, more significantly, established disparities in spending per pupil as high as 8:1 in comparison between similarly sized school districts." The court agreed with expert testimony that established a positive correlation between funding levels and equality of educational opportunity.

The Montana Supreme Court found that the state educational delivery system did not provide equality of educational opportunity as a result of significant differences in per pupil spending across school districts. Unchallenged expert testimony found that the Montana foundation program fell short of meeting the costs of compliance with the state minimum accreditation standards. The court held that the state education system failed to provide all students with equality of educational opportunity as required by the state constitution.

The Kentucky Case

In what could become a landmark decision, the Kentucky Supreme Court ruled that the state legislature did not comply with the constitutional mandate to provide an efficient state system of common schools (*Rose v. Council for Better Education*, 1989). The plaintiff, the Council for Better Education, argued that the method of financing for public schools provided by the state general assembly was insufficient because it relied too heavily on the resources of local school boards. The legal relief sought legislation that would require an "equitable and adequate funding program for all school children so as to establish an efficient system of common schools" throughout the state of Kentucky. The court found that students enrolled in "property poor" districts were getting inferior and inadequate education compared with their counterparts in wealthier school districts.

The court based its findings on legislative history to declare unilaterally that public education is a constitutional right in the State of Kentucky. It further concluded that the system of common schools must be sufficiently financed to ensure that all the state's public school children are afforded an equal opportunity for an adequate education. It ordered the general assembly to determine how to achieve an efficient system to meet these goals.

The Kentucky Supreme Court went much further, however, and mandated that the educational delivery system devised by the legislature and appropriate state agencies must include the following seven specific goals:

1. Sufficient oral and written communication skills to enable students to function in a complex and rapidly changing civilization
2. Sufficient knowledge of economic, social, and political systems to enable each student to make informed choices
3. Sufficient understanding of governmental processes to enable all students to understand the public issues that affect their community
4. Sufficient self-knowledge and knowledge of his or her mental and physical wellness
5. Sufficient grounding in the arts to enable all students to appreciate their cultural and historical legacies
6. Sufficient training in either academic or vocational fields so as to enable each student to choose and find work successfully and intelligently
7. Sufficient levels of these skills to enable all public school students to compete equally and favorably in the job market with their fellow students in surrounding states

In perhaps the most sweeping of the state financing decisions, the court ordered the Kentucky General Assembly to re-create the funding system for public elementary and secondary education to meet constitutional standards. Specifically, under the revamped system, each school district was to be adequately funded; tax rates on personal and real property were to be uniformly established and enforced; and for tax purposes, property, as a source of local revenues for public schools, was to be assessed at 100 percent of fair market value.

The Texas Case

The Texas Supreme Court held that the method of financing public education was unconstitutional. In *Edgewood Independent School District v. Kirby* (1989), the court relied on evidence that found financing disparities resulting in a 700:1 ratio of property wealth per capita in the most affluent school districts compared with the poorest districts. Per capita spending varied enormously, ranging from a high of $19,333 per pupil to a low of $2,112 per pupil. Based on these data, the Supreme Court of Texas, as did the courts in Montana and

Kentucky, found correlations between unequal per pupil spending and unequal educational opportunity for a substantial number of the state's public school children.

Moreover, the court noted that the state funding formula for allocating additional funding for poor school districts to compensate for disparities in wealth was not adequate to cover the cost of meeting minimum educational standards. The court therefore concluded that the state public school system was not efficient with respect to both school finance and the general diffusion of knowledge.

The Texas court concluded that additional funding awarded in a piecemeal fashion was not sufficient to make the education system truly efficient. It ruled that the entire system must be scrapped and changed immediately. Unlike the actions of the Supreme Court in Kentucky, however, the Texas court decided against ordering the legislature to include specific standards in the new delivery system, although it did establish as a general criterion a direct correlation between a school district's tax effort and the level of local educational resources available to meet the new requirements that the legislature would ultimately agree on.

The New Jersey Case

The New Jersey situation was specifically concerned with the importance of equity in determining whether or not students from poor urban school districts were educationally discriminated against and hence legally entitled to special treatment under the state constitution. The New Jersey State Supreme Court ruled in *Abbott v. Burke* (1990) that the Public Education Act and the minimum finance formula were both unconstitutional. Plaintiffs included students from the cities of Camden, East Orange, and Jersey City, who contended that the act violated the "thorough and efficient" clause of the state constitution. The supreme court held that the education finance system was neither thorough nor efficient and, specifically, that the act was unconstitutional with regard to poor urban school districts in New Jersey. The court found that a thorough and efficient system would give at-risk students an opportunity equal to that of more advantaged students.

Data gathered by the plaintiffs established that the disparities in funding and expenditures actually had increased since passage of the act; that a positive relationship existed between the per capita income levels of the local school districts and the per pupil expenditure level, and that the more urban the district, the heavier its municipal property tax and the greater the school tax burden. These findings led to the court's conclusion that the system of public school finance was unconstitutional with respect to urban school districts.

The disparities in per pupil expenditures between relatively poor urban districts and more affluent ones revealed an inadequate system of funding and an inadequate quality of education in urban districts. More dramatically, these deficiences in poor urban districts were illustrated by the lack of educational opportunities in areas such as science, biology, foreign languages, music, art, industrial arts, physical education, computer education, and special education. Many of these curricular offerings (e.g., art instruction) were mandated by the Kentucky court.

In addition, the court found what observers of public urban education had long recognized. The conditions of the physical facilities in inner-city schools were abysmal when compared with those in more affluent suburban districts. Pupil-teacher ratios, years of teaching experience, average length of education of teachers—all improved relative to a district's wealth in property, average per pupil expenditures, and socioeconomic status. The court record clearly indicated that the educational needs of schoolchildren in urban districts vastly exceeded those of other students, notably those enrolled in schools located in more affluent communities. Moreover, the needs of urban children extended beyond educational needs to include basic essentials such as food, clothing, and housing as well as social needs such as close family and community bonds. The New Jersey Supreme Court found that these unmet needs for inner-city schoolchildren stemmed from living for extended periods of time in a social environment marked by violence, poverty, and human misery.

The most significant court finding for our purposes stated that the state system of public elementary and secondary education should motivate urban schoolchildren to excel in school and provide educational opportunities that would enable at-risk students to take advantage of their innate capacity to learn. The court further noted that schoolchildren in inner-city schools needed much more than the schools were giving them to achieve the thorough and efficient requirements of the state constitution. If more money was not a panacea for solving these problems, the court reasoned, additional funding was nevertheless essential to help the children who were constitutionally entitled to that assistance. Consistent with remedies in other state court decisions cited above, the court allowed the state legislature to establish the finance mechanism to produce a more equitable educational opportunity for at-risk students.

This nationwide trend to declare state finance formulas unconstitutional because of the failure to affect a thorough and efficient system of public elementary and secondary education obviously has broad policy implications for local school boards. Before we can begin to understand the impact of state finance decisions on the governance and policy roles of school boards, it would be helpful to turn to the theoretical literature to conceptualize these roles. From there, we can analyze the range of alternative responses to state finance decisions by school boards within this theoretical framework. The next section examines the theoretical literature on the roles of school boards as mechanisms of the state and their relationship to the function of schools in postindustrial economies.

SCHOOL BOARD POLICYMAKING

Models of Educational Policymaking

In his now classic study of educational policymaking in Chicago, Paul Peterson (1976) views the policymaking system as an interrelationship between two models: a unitary model and a bargaining model. Central to the bargaining model is a pluralistic perspective that views "public policy [as] formulated through bargaining and negotiation among a plurality of individual groups, agencies, and interests." Peterson's work broke new theoretical ground in the application of pluralism to educational policymaking by distinguishing between pluralistic bargaining and ideological bargaining. According to Peterson, pluralistic bargaining involves the preservation and enhancement of an individual actor's narrow "immediate electoral or organizational interests." Ideological bargaining, on the other hand, takes place when actors are emotionally and ideologically wedded to a broader range of policy issues such as school choice. Peterson notes that those policy issues "are regarded as of such an enduring significance that the participant becomes deeply, ideologically, committed to them" (p. xii).

Ideological bargaining obviously provokes intense conflict in comparison to pluralistic bargaining, where policymaking consists of frequent compromise with a changing alliance of electoral and policy groups. Although Peterson thoroughly distinguishes between these two variants of bargaining models, the overriding theoretical concern is with the policymaking processes of the Chicago School Board (during the administration of Superintendent James Redmond) as it engaged in conflict and compromise with a plethora of external constituents and a united set of administrators. These processes are shaped by theoretical and normative judgments, which view the political system as an "arena" wherein "a competitive struggle between such interest groups over the scarce distribution of tangible goods" and services is played out (Smith, 1974, p. 111).

The unitary models postulating a "single set of factors" constrain the ability of local school boards to consider a range of policy proposals. These sets of constraints may flow from two sources: (1) the internal organization within the school system, that is, its singular interests, values, and standard operating procedures; and (2) the school board members "as rational, value-maximizing, goal-oriented decisionmakers" (Peterson, 1976, p. xiii). Whereas bargaining models assume that policy is the outcome of pluralistic or ideological bargaining, the unitary models postulate an underlying unity within the policymaking system. Both bargaining and unitary models assume that the policy system is a neutral arena where bargaining deals are struck among equally competing interest groups.

By contrast, revisionist pluralist theorists have focused attention on the inherent bias and "preferred access" of the policymaking system (Smith, 1974, p. 24), which cuts against the normative pluralists' assumptions of equally competing interest groups in a neutral arena. Smith applied this revisionist perspective to a study of local school board educational policymaking in suburban settings.

Smith described how professional administrators captured control over educational policymaking in suburban Massachusetts, where an ethos of "community conservation" prevailed. This model of political behavior in local education settings views interest group bargaining and compromise, whether pluralistic or ideological, "as an illegitimate mode of policy formation" (p. 112). Unlike the models of policymaking embedded in Peterson's notion of pluralistic and ideological bargaining, the managerial view regards educational policymaking as the central role of local school boards.

School boards are often constrained in their attempts to address the central purposes of schooling in their policymaking. Demands that boards attend to noninstructional areas of district upkeep direct the attention of boards away from policymaking directly connected to the functions of schools.

Views of the Functions of Schools

What do schools actually do? This question has been pondered by education theorists from conservative, liberal, and radical ideological perspectives. Schools obviously serve as instructional sites where the "core" technical activities of teaching and learning occur. Much reform activity and criticism of the performance of schools has been aimed at the failure of local school boards to induce competitive academic performance within public schools. Local school boards have been perceived as failing institutions because as guardians of the public trust, they have not accounted efficiently for tax dollars meant to be used for achieving academic excellence.

Michael Apple (1982) theorizes a role for schools, as cultural apparati of the state, that places the instructional function of the schools in political and economic perspective. Apple argues that schools may be understood as the means of both "amelioration" and "problem solving" for individual students who strive to become upwardly mobile. Thus, the instructional role of the school, which assists students in "getting ahead" in life socially and economically, is not separate from the role of the school in shaping who gets ahead and the groups of individuals who benefit from schooling.

This essentially "contradictory" role of the schools—their capacity to assist individual students while systematically "sorting" and "selecting" (McLaren, 1989; Apple, 1988) groups of students into the existing social division of labor—points to the theoretical role of public schools in postindustrial societies. Apple (1988) asserts that schools, as units of the state, serve three noninstructional purposes: accumulation, legitimation, and production (1988, pp. 192–195). By extension, local school boards, having been delegated governance responsibilities over public education by state constitutions, are perceived as the public (in many cases, elected) body that is held accountable to fulfill these purposes. Although these purposes of the school are analytically distinct from instructional functions, they are inextricably bound to the instructional mission of the school, viewed here as a social organization that serves as host site for cultural as well as instructional activity (Giroux, 1983).

Accumulation. Through their capacity to sort and select students internally according to "talent," schools help dominant economic groups to accumulate capital (Apple, 1988, p. 193). Therefore, the "conditions for recreating an unequally responsive economy" are achieved in the schools in part through the technical features of instruction and through the form of the curriculum itself. In the case of the state "bankruptcy" statutes, school boards are widely perceived as having completely abdicated their responsibility of ensuring an entry-level workforce that is capable of providing labor, manpower, and problem-solving skills needed for the "information age." The failure of local school boards to demand minimum satisfactory achievement has dire consequences for the economy. Labor costs rise as more expensive personnel have to be hired from out of state; or training budgets escalate as business and industry need to retrain employees.

Legitimation. Second, schools serve a legitimation function. They accomplish this by providing an organizational structure to legitimize the knowledge, values, and cultural tastes of certain social groups. While schools marginalize other groups (for example, students with limited English proficiency), they reproduce and sustain cultural ideologies such as meritocracy and fairness in order to justify the unequal outcomes. Thus, local school boards are in fact constrained in their abilities to enact school policies and programs such as teacher and student empowerment because they do not want to work against the mythology of merit and equal treatment for all groups.

Production. Third, schools support a production function by their capacity to instill in students technical/administrative knowledge and ideologies. Local school districts seem enamored, for example, with increasing the emphasis on mathematics and science instruction. Schools assist in the production of knowledge needed to expand existing markets and to create new ones, stimulate consumer "needs," and maintain, and thus control, the existing division of labor. Also relevant here is the school's role in the production of "technicist ideologies," which when coupled with school practices, have the effect of reducing "the cultural sphere (sphere of democratic discourse and shared understanding) to the application of technical rules and procedure" (Apple, 1988, p. 194).

Despite the control of billions of dollars of public money at the local

level, the ability of school boards to govern effectively is greatly
constrained by the technical and ideological function of the schools.
In large measure, the governance of public elementary and secondary
education by local school boards is a political role that is inextricably
tied to the structural role of schools as economic and cultural institutions of the state. The source of the "power" of school boards can be
defined as both legal authority and decision-making capacity over the
instructional domain of schools. Within this historical and theoretical
framework, we now turn to consider the array of local board responses
to the wave of legal challenges to state finance formulas and other
statutory tests (e.g., academic "bankruptcy") of governance.

Views of the Roles of Boards

From the discussion above, we can envision several interrelated
roles that local school boards may assume. These are satisficer
(Simon, 1957), legitimator, patronizer, bargainer, and policymaker.
The satisfying school board is the "value-maximizing" actor, which
Peterson describes as compromising the rational-actor view of educational policymaking. Here the role of the school board is to establish
school policy as incrementally as possible, giving utmost attention to
such overriding community needs as maintaining harmonious race
relations or guarding the economic interest of the school system. The
legitimating school board borrows from Smith's notion of "managerial" political culture and poses a board whose primary function is to
serve as "ceremonial policymaker" (Smith, 1974, p. 127). The superintendent and his or her staff dominate policymaking and expect the
school board to engage in democratic rituals to give legitimacy to
predetermined policy. Following Peterson, the bargaining school
board pluralistically bargains with an array of equally competing
interest groups over narrow, relatively short-term issues or mediates
ideological conflict between groups on a number of limited, but emotional, issues. The patronizer engages primarily in the awarding of
school board contracts to provide goods and services for the school
district. Since school systems constitute a "purveyor" (Cuban, 1983),
the local school board seizes these resources as a source of patronage
to garner electoral support for future campaigns or to enlist constit-
uent support through patronage contracts during heated policy debate. The policymaker role stems from the board's legal authority to

enact rules and regulations to implement the intent of legislation or of policies of the state board of education.

These roles are not "ideal" types in that we see plenty of overlap among the categories. For instance, the satisficer role and the legitimator role are closely related inasmuch as both stress the incremental nature of school board policymaking. The distinction is that the satisficer role of the school board is embedded in preserving an overriding unified interest, whereas the legitimator role stems from the "preferred access" position of the district's administrative staff. In general terms, we view school board members as moving from less to more proactive roles in the formulation of educational policy. We view the content of this policy as moving from statements of the instrumental function of schools as economic and political agents of the state to statements that could potentially liberate schools as cultural sites where the entire school community of professionals, students, parents, and neighborhood people could engage in democratic processes to meet shared purposes. We now examine the array of potential choices available to school boards in light of the theoretical categories we have postulated.

SCHOOL BOARD ROLES IN ACTION

As Satisficer

With new funding formulas, school boards are in a much different policy environment from that which existed under old finance arrangements. For example, the urban school district of New Orleans, with a 90 percent minority enrollment and almost the same percentage of students on free and reduced-price lunch programs, can expect up to $42 million more in state funding under changes in the minimum foundation formula being considered in 1991 by the Louisiana State Board of Elementary and Secondary Education. These funds would eliminate the estimated $12 million shortfall for the next fiscal year and provide much needed support for the district's abysmally low $32 per pupil funding for texts and materials.

As in most districts, even poor urban ones, there are disparities in funding levels within the New Orleans district. Parents in wealthier neighborhoods in Orleans Parish, for instance, routinely raise as much as $50,000 in extramural funds to support their children's schools. On the other hand, inner-city parent groups often have trouble raising $500 annually for extra supplies and programs. Faced with the prospects of additional funding, school boards in "property-poor districts" could simply satisfy all their constituents evenly by dividing up the total pool of funds and distributing them "across the board" without regard to individual school needs.

Similarly, a more affluent district, faced with budget cuts from the state, could simply reduce funding equally for all schools. This response in more affluent districts has less obvious unanticipated negative consequences in that there is a substantially lower number of schools in financial jeopardy.

These two contexts for school board policymaking—relatively poor urban districts and more affluent ones—also can be applied to our second category of action, bargaining.

As Bargainer

School boards in urban districts are more likely to bargain with electoral constituents than are school boards in suburban affluent districts. Another example drawn from the New Orleans school district, which has recently endured a fourth teachers' strike in fifteen years, serves to illustrate our argument.

As part of the settlement contract with the United Teachers of New Orleans, management and labor agreed to a provision that teachers would not mobilize to recall individual school board members. They also agreed that, in addition to salary increases for teachers and paraprofessionals, the district would also grant raises to the administrators in the school system—a move that would increase the cost of the settlement by approximately $800,000. When confronted by informed and upset parent groups, however, the board "bargained" with both the parents and the superintendent's cabinet to exclude the pay raises for upper-level administrators. Such an outcome is likely in an urban context where a change in finances has been ordered by a state court. Bargaining is less likely in affluent suburban districts where an ethos of professionalism relegates the school board's role to ceremony and a legitimator of policies advanced by the superintendent and the central office staff (Smith, 1974).

As Legitimizer

School boards are likely to defer to the professional judgment of the superintendent when faced with major changes in school finance formulas, which in turn would necessitate policy change. Major state finance rulings handed down by state supreme courts are unlikely to have a substantial effect on school boards in affluent districts or on board members in urban districts whose constituents conduct campaigns to raise monies in the amounts noted above. Both types of board members are likely to serve as legitimating agents for policy decisions made by the central office, or advanced by school-level personnel.

It is unlikely, given the pluralistic nature of local educational policymaking, that school boards in financially strapped urban districts would ceremoniously legitimize administrative policy. If legitimation roles do emerge, it is more plausible that boards in these districts would give legitimacy to previously disenfranchised constituents who have been locked out of the policy process. Again, evidence is emerging in Louisiana to confirm that school boards are more likely to provide a legitimate voice for electoral constituents rather than for a superintendent and his or her professional staff. Nonetheless, a bargaining posture is more likely in urban districts and a legitimation role more probable in affluent suburban districts.

As Patronizer

The most likely role for school boards under revamped finance formulas is a patronage role. As economic agents of the state, schools assist in accumulation, legitimation, and production functions (Apple, 1982). More money coming into school districts, whether urban or rural, means more contract money for school boards as purveyors of goods and services. Even in relatively affluent districts, we suspect that school boards are likely to seek to bargain with the superintendent and the professional staff or possibly with the legislature for the purpose of continuing the board's patronage role with local contractors. In this context, therefore, the school board's patronage role is interwoven with a bargaining role more characteristic of boards in urban districts and in tightly knit rural communities. The interconnecting nature of school board roles is most evident when patronage opportunities are rampant as a result of increased funding, or more subtly, when those traditions are easily threatened because of losses in state funds. Examples include lucrative legal contracts in large urban districts where legal problems are part of everyday school life.

As Policymaker

The most problematic role of local school boards is that of educational policymaker. As Peterson's (1976) unitary model of local policy formation informs us, school boards are dependent on the superintendent and the administrative office for data and information for making data-based decisions that are not simply knee-jerk emotional reactions to constituents' demands. In addition, local school districts are constrained by the overriding interests of the communities in which they reside; for example, in promoting and achieving economic growth and in maintaining harmonious race relations. As elected or appointed officials, school board members must also give attention to the cost of running in future elections, or to paying back previous campaign debts, as well as being loyal to the mayor or nominating committees who appointed them to office.

School boards, therefore, need an effective constituency in order to engage in substantive educational policymaking that is independent of administrative information and mindful of, though not overreactive to, the political/economic structure of the community. Parents of public school children have often served as that support group as well as a constructive source of criticism that can move school boards beyond their narrow "bargaining" and "patronage" roles to policymakers in the public interest. "Apple Corps" in Atlanta and "Jacksonians for Better Schools" are two visible parent groups that have gained national attention by their promotional activities in support of quality public schools and their "watchdog" role as monitors of school boards.

We assert that in times of crisis such as the wave of recent state finance decisions cited above, local school boards can recapture their policymaking role as it was envisioned by the educational reformers of the 1930s who wanted to "take politics out of education" by eliminating the influence of ward-based politics in school board elections. As political scientists have long established, this idealistic scenario is at best difficult to achieve and at worst naive about the nature of educational policy. With the help of parents of school-age children, school boards can establish broad educational goals and measurable objectives that can be used to evaluate the effectiveness of teaching and learning. These goals and objectives can then be used to make informed judgments as to where new monies should be targeted or cuts should be made. Illustrations from recent crisis situations and proposed legal challenges to the minimum foundation formula in Louisiana highlight how parent groups and others can assist school boards in assuming a meaningful policy role.

The New Orleans Public Schools recently endured the longest teacher strike in the district's history, in which 60 to 70 percent of the teachers walked out and several incidents occurred involving unqualified teachers. The strike was ultimately settled at a projected cost to the district of $6 million to finance pay raises for teachers, clerical workers, and maintenance personnel covered by the bargaining unit, the United Teachers of New Orleans (UTNO). The administration had proposed to finance the additional raises for administrators by cutting important school programs and eliminating all elementary librarians and social workers. Although the news media widely reported that these raises for administrative staff were in fact part of the teachers' bargaining contract, parent groups pointed out that the school board would have to ratify them in a separate vote and that the raises were not covered by the written agreements eventually ratified by UTNO. The school board rescinded the pay hikes for central office administrators, siding with the parents who argued that it would be morally irresponsible to finance more money for central office staff at the expense of student programs. Previously, several school board members privately disclosed to parents that the raises for administrators was a "done deal" and that nothing short of a political miracle would stop them.

Finally, law professors, civic groups, and parents were working in the early 1990s with "property-poor" school districts in Louisiana to garner public support for the proposed changes in the minimum foundation formula, which would result in significant new funds for urban school districts. In New Orleans, it has been estimated that such revisions would net an extra $42 million, an increase in the operating budget of about 15 percent. These groups were working to pressure the school boards to increase the per pupil spending for books and supplies and to implement innovative site-based management schemes. Without such grass-roots interest, we predict that school boards in Louisiana and other states across the country will fall back on less proactive roles in the setting of school priorities that would establish the framework for spending new monies.

SUMMARY AND CONCLUSIONS

In this chapter, we have demonstrated how the historical development of state funding of public elementary education in the United
States has, *ipso facto*, created a mechanism whereby local school
districts are controlled by the state. The role assumed by local school
boards in the governance of education is dependent on its financial
relationship to the state. Moreover, school boards are vulnerable to
the vicissitudes of state finance and accountability schemes, as is
evidenced by recent decisions of state supreme courts to restructure
funding formulas and mandate curriculum and outcome standards in
local school districts.

The unresolved tensions between the state and the broader local
communities, which school boards are either elected or appointed to
represent, continue to plague the issue of governance in general and
limit the substantive role of school boards in educational policymaking in particular. Also, a growing trend toward private sector involvement in public education, through "partnership" agreements such as
that between the Chelsea school district and Boston University has
the potential to reconfigure the governance of public education at the
local level and cause school boards to be accountable to private rather
than public interests.

In the final analysis, the philosophical and political questions that
undergirded the development of public schooling, such as conflicts
between community (the people) and the state, remain embedded in
the forces that are working to redefine, and perhaps even eliminate,
school boards as policymaking institutions. Such an outcome is consistent with the theoretical work of Michael Apple (1982), who contends that schools actually serve the economic interest of the state. It
should be noted that both the interest in the state to force outcome
changes through revamped funding schemes and privatization trends
support accumulation "needs."

We suggest that placing these contemporary conflicts in historical,
philosophical, and theoretical perspective can, at minimum, inform
our understanding about the policy implications and actions state
activity compels. Optimistically, such a broad understanding maxi-
mizes the range of viable political choices we as a society can make.
These contemporary issues affecting local school boards are variations
of the old themes: Who controls public education? Who are the
"publics" that education seeks to serve?

REFERENCES

Abbott v. Burke, 575 A. 2d 359 (N.J. 1990).

Apple, Michael. *Education and Power: Reproduction and Contradiction in Education.* Boston: Routledge Chapman and Hall, 1982.

Apple, Michael. "Social Crisis and Curriculum Accord," *Educational Policy* 38, no. 2 (1988): 191–201.

Butts, Robert Freeman, and Cremin, Lawrence Arthur. *A History of Education in American Culture.* New York: Holt, Rinehart and Winston, 1953.

Cremin, Lawrence Arthur. *American Education: The Colonial Experience, 1607–1783.* New York: Harper and Row, 1970.

Cuban, Larry. "Corporate Involvement in Public Schools: A Practitioner-Academic's Perspective," *Teachers College Record* 85, no. 2 (1983): 183–203.

Cubberley, Ellwood P. *Public Education in the United States: A Study and Interpretation of American Educational History.* Boston: Houghton Mifflin, 1919.

Edgewood Independent School District v. Kirby, 777 S.W. 2d 391 (Tex. 1989).

Giroux, Henry A. *Theory and Resistance in Education.* South Hadley, Mass.: Bergin and Garvey, 1983.

Helena Elementary School District No. 1 v. The State of Montana, 784 p. 2d 412 (Mont. 1990).

Hubsch, Allen W. "Education and Self-Government: The Right to Education under State Constitutional Law," *Journal of Law and Education* 18 (Winter 1989): 93–142.

McLaren, Peter. *Life in Schools: An Introduction to Critical Pedagogy in the Foundations of Education.* New York: Longman, 1989.

Peterson, Paul E. *School Politics Chicago Style.* Chicago: University of Chicago Press, 1976.

Rose v. Council for Better Education, Inc., 790 S.W. 2d 186 (Ky. 1989).

Simon, Herbert. *Administrative Behavior.* New York: Macmillan, 1957.

Smith, Michael P. "The Ritual Politics of Suburban Schools." In *Politics in America*, edited by Michael P. Smith, pp. 110–126. New York: Random House, 1974.

Thompson, David C. "School Finance Litigation: A Rising Concern," *NOLPE Notes*, 25, no. 1 (1990): 1–3.

Welter, Rush. *Popular Education and Democratic Thought in America.* New York: Columbia University Press, 1962.

CHAPTER 9

Evaluating School Boards: Looking Through Next-Generation Lenses

Patricia F. First

Local school boards were largely neglected during the 1980s—the decade of educational reform. Simultaneously and in waves, the reform efforts increased both the centralization to the state level and decentralization to the school level of the governance and decision-making authority (Boyd, 1990). The board level, the level between state and school, was bypassed. Even in studies of local response to state and federal reform efforts, the focus was on leadership at the district and school-site levels, but not on boards as boards (Odden and Marsh, 1990). The third wave of educational reform (federal leadership, national goals, national testing, de facto national curriculum) seems destined to remove any reform focus still further from local boards of education. In the 1990s, thinking about the usefulness of local boards of education is polarized. Some see local boards as modern-day dinosaurs and others see local boards as a symbol of democracy in action. (See Chapters 2 and 3 in this volume.) And some look toward a new balance of control and autonomy: "Schools, school districts and their boards, and state departments and state boards of education need one another; none are likely to be complete and adequate without the other" (Boyd, 1990, p. 88).

Local school boards are probably a little bit of both dinosaur and democratic symbol, but before taking either position, it would be profitable to think about some evaluation of the functioning of local boards separate from leadership in general at the school district level. Talking evaluation is talking a political process, a value-laden process, a controversial process. What could be more appropriately applied to the local school board than a political, value-laden, controversial process?

There is no question that school boards have absorbed much criticism in recent years. Some, maybe most of it, is deserved. But my argument in this chapter is that something good may also be happening with local school boards. The general public thinks that having local school boards to look after their children's interests is important, though they often admit to an unclear view of what the school board really does or should be doing (Institute for Educational Leadership, 1986). It is possible that both critics and advocates are looking at school boards through out-of-date lenses—that something positive is happening with school boards, but that we need a fresh approach to discern what it is.

The key might be to look at school boards through "next-generation" lenses, to look at these entities as the crew of the Starship Enterprise might look at them if school boards were encountered while the crew members were star trekking about the galaxies on a mission of exploration. In such an encounter, there would be no preconceived notions such as the idea that these school boards should be making policy. The next-generation crew would observe school boards as they found them and seek to understand what these boards were contributing to their society. On the way to suggesting how we might step back, disengage, and look at school boards in a fresh way, other topics will be discussed here. We will look at evaluation as a political process and at some of the ways boards are now evaluated. We will briefly examine what we think boards do and describe some of the past studies on boards. And we will look at the changing demographics of U.S. society, which school boards are attempting to serve. And last, we will return to the notion of looking at boards with a fresh approach through "next-generation lenses."

EVALUATION AS A POLITICAL PROCESS

Some would argue that a school board cannot be effectively evaluated because of the political overtones to both the entity and the process. Eleanor Chelimsky (1987) wrote of the "very difficult problem of integrating the disparate worlds of politics and evaluation research" (p. 200). We agree instead with George Noblit and Deborah Eaker (1989) that "politics and evaluation research, although giving the impression of disparate worlds, are instead inextricably linked, . . . that not only the outcomes of evaluation, but the evaluation process itself is political and the decision to subject a program and its participants to evaluation is a policy decision" (p. 127).

Few local school boards have made the policy decision to subject themselves to the political process of evaluation. And on what would they be evaluated? Their roles are many and few agree on them, even board members themselves. Boards may have good reason to fear formal evaluation processes. A good evaluation has the power to realign political power, and this is what boards seem to fear. Ninety-five percent of local school board members are, after all, elected to their positions. In the value-laden choice making of the evaluation design process, bases for judgment by others and by the board members themselves are established. Other possible bases for judgment are discarded or demoted to a lesser significance. But agreeing that evaluations are political and that they may understandably be feared is not to agree that evaluations are unworthy social processes. On the contrary, evaluations can be worthy and publicly recognized processes through which values and worthiness are created (Noblit and Eaker, 1989). Many local school boards would be grateful for such public validation of their worthiness.

PRESENT CONSTRAINTS ON AND EVALUATIONS OF THE WORK OF LOCAL SCHOOL BOARDS

There are many reasons why it is difficult to evaluate the functioning of local school boards. Given our intergovernmental system for governing education, boards are not free to exercise unfettered discretion on behalf of their local constituencies. They must act within the parameters established by the state. In the reform decade of the 1980s, we saw the specificity of the state parameters increase. We also need to remember that although the Tenth Amendment to the Constitution gives primary responsibility for the governance of education to the respective states, federal involvement is not precluded. In the decades since *Brown v. Board of Education* in 1954, the federal presence on behalf of access to education and civil rights has set further operating parameters for the work of the local school board. (The value judgment about the necessity of these federal and state constraints is not the point here. This is simply a reminder that other influences, particularly statutes and court decisions, must be remembered in any evaluation design.)

State constitutions vest total control over education in their legislatures, and there are generally no limits on the legislative control of education. But within the limits of any state legislature's delegation, local boards have implied power to act as they deem appropriate in matters of educational policy and school governance. Clearly there is room for an evaluative scheme even with all the caveats and constraints stated above.

State agencies, acting for state boards of education in all but one state, perform audits and other forms of evaluation of local school districts and thus, by association, of local school boards. There has been much publicity about the ultimate "big stick"—the state takeover—if a school board is found terribly wanting in the state's criteria of adequacy. The takeover of Jersey City by the state agency in New Jersey is a late-1980s example of this penalty in effect. (See Chapter 5 in this volume.) A state takeover is an action taken by the state when it determines, through a deliberate review and progressively intrusive process, that the school district cannot or will not meet prescribed standards. When such a penalty is inflicted, an advisory board from the local community may be appointed by the chief state school officer to replace the sitting local school board. This is obviously an enormous penalty and surely an example of evaluation at work. But it is such a huge penalty, analogous to the withdrawal of federal funds from an entire institution if there is a civil rights violation in any of the institution's programs, that a school district/school board must be utterly awful, and utterly awful over a very long period of time before the penalty is inflicted. This is a crude form of evaluation, appropriate only for the worst of educational circumstances. It gives us no clues on how to evaluate a board that wishes to strive for excellence and is doing a good job.

The courts are frequently cited as a constraining influence on the actions of the local school board. But the courts do not ordinarily interfere with the actions of a school board unless there is a clear abuse of discretion or a violation of the law. The courts typically review the processes by which a board makes its decision rather than the educational decision itself.

The courts are not likely to intervene if a school board properly exercises those narrowly defined powers expressly delegated to it by law, or acts in a manner that is reasonably implied by the law or is incidental to this authority, or acts in a fashion that is essential to the accomplishment of the objectives of its schools. All of which says that just staying out of trouble with the law or with the courts, which sometimes seems to be the actual goal of school board choices and actions, does not indicate in any way if the board is performing well on any criteria of excellence or even adequacy. It certainly gives no indication of whether or not the board is exerting leadership at any level in determining that each child in its care is provided with a good education and thus good life chances.

SYSTEMS IN USE FOR THE EVALUATION OF SCHOOL BOARDS

There have been a number of instruments developed through the years for the evaluation and/or self-evaluation of school boards. In 1980, the American Association of School Administrators (AASA) and the National School Boards Association (NSBA) issued a joint publication, *Goal Setting and Self-Evaluation of School Boards*. Using a three-point scale of adequate, inadequate, and how to improve, school boards can evaluate their performance in their traditional areas of responsibility: instructional program, students, basic commitments, board operations, relationship with the superintendent, fiscal management, noninstructional services, facilities, personnel, employer-employee relations, and school-community relations. The authoring organizations suggest that boards evaluate themselves at least once a year and promulgate a policy statement concerning self-evaluation, such as "The board believes that periodic formal and informal evaluations of its operational procedures will improve the board's performance, exemplify the kind of constructive evaluations the board encourages for all school personnel and programs, and promote a spirit of teamwork throughout the district. Formal evaluations also provide the board with suggestions useful to the board in establishing objectives it will strive to accomplish" (AASA/NSBA, 1980, p. 3).

In the late 1980s, the Institute for Educational Leadership (IEL) developed a self-assessment system for school boards that provided for comprehensive self-assessment and incorporated strategies to help boards act on the results of their assessments. IEL hoped to promote widespread board self-assessment and follow-up development activities to improve school board effectiveness. (See Chapter 6 in this volume.) The complete system takes a board from the actual self-assessment on a six-point rating scale through the development of a written self-improvement plan. There are fifteen areas of board activity covered in the evaluation: leadership, communications, parent and community involvement, influence on others, decision making, planning and goal setting, resource allocation, policy development, policy oversight, selection and evaluation of the superintendent, working with the superintendent, employee relations, expectations for board member conduct, board operations, and board development.

Late-1980s reforms have emphasized the expertise of teachers and the input of parents and teachers in the governance of education. In seeking to evaluate their school boards, some communities have designed systems and/or instruments that reflect this emphasis on input from the board's constituencies. In New Orleans, for example, a reform group designed a community report card for the school board (Garvin, 1991). Using a six-point scale from strongly disagree to strongly agree, responders are asked to rate the board on eight categories: understands educational leadership; provides educational leadership; expresses leadership by allowing parent/community and teacher involvement and displaying the ability to make choices of conscience versus choices of politics; communicates with community, parents, and teachers; shows flexibility in planning and goal setting; sets plans and goals after input from community, parents, and teachers; follows its plans and goals; and assesses progress in an informed and enlightened manner, taking into consideration community and parental expectations, teacher resources, and the learning environment of the student.

Such an instrument clearly reflects a belief in the importance of input from constituents and the value of responsiveness to the community. It is still, however, an evaluation of process. We are no closer to a "bottom line," no closer to evaluating the quality of board decisions as they relate to what is best for children. There is an assumption in many of the newer systems for evaluating school boards that the more the board listens and the more people and groups it listens to, the more the quality of board decisions will improve.

One of the reforms that has brought the role of school boards to public discussion is school-based management. Once we acknowledge that the important decisions should be made at the school site, the question is asked: What remains of the need for a school district and what remains for a district school board to do? We have a description of the role of the board in the management plan in the Edmonton Public School District in Alberta, Canada. The role of the board, now that school-based management has evolved for ten years, is the following:

> The elected school board sets priorities each year which must be addressed in all schools. Budget preparation and staff selection are wholly decentralized to schools. Accountability in an education sense is addressed through a system-wide set of standardized tests in language, mathematics, science, and social studies at two points in elementary schooling and at one point in secondary. Target levels of performance are set each year. [Boyd, 1990, p. 91]

In a situation such as this, one of the process systems of evaluations could be used to determine how the board set the yearly priorities. But to really learn about the quality of the schooling provided by the board rather than the processes that the board uses to provide schooling, a simple evaluation could be used, such as that suggested by the Organization for Economic Cooperation and Development (1987). Three basic questions are asked about the board: Does the board set quality targets and provide the means of attaining them? Does the board monitor the implementation of appropriate strategies? Does the board conduct regular appraisals of performance in association with the schools concerned? The point here is to evaluate the results, not to manage or control. Obviously, these questions are harder to answer than the process questions. It is far easier for board members to know that they have provided opportunity for community involvement than it is for them to know whether or not the best and most appropriate learning techniques are being used for the children in their district. But when all is said and done, is it not the board's business to know the answers to these hard questions? As John Carver (1990) puts it, boards that make a difference redefine excellence in governance and invent new strategies for board leadership. Such boards "are obsessed with effects for people" (p. 193).

WHAT SCHOOL BOARDS REALLY DO

Among thoughtful people, there are wide-ranging differences of opinion regarding the efficacy and importance of the local school board. That school boards waste their time on trivial matters has become a stereotype. Anne C. Lewis (1988), in lamenting the lack of exciting public debate about education, states bluntly, "School boards tend to concern themselves with trivia" (p. 324). Denis Doyle, communicating directly with boards via the *American School Board Journal*, says, "No corporation could run for a week with the kind of niggling oversight school boards habitually practice" (as quoted in Reecer, 1989, p. 34).

But others still see the local school board as an important, if neglected, link in the governance of education. As Nellie C. Weil, President of the National School Boards Association, pointed out in 1986, "Improvement in the instructional program, to be truly effective, needs the support of the people in the local communities. Those people look to their local school boards for leadership in this task. Therefore, state efforts to improve education must involve school boards as an integral part of the process" (Institute for Educational Leadership, 1986, p. iii). Marcia Reecer's panel of school board watchers suggested to boards that they do more looking outward, more representing of education to the community, and more linking with the growing segments of the population not directly connected to the public schools (Reecer, 1989).

In 1989, Jeri Nowakowski and Patricia First reported on a study of twelve Illinois school districts in the aftermath of the 1985 Illinois reform legislation. After reading and analyzing three years of board minutes in these twelve districts, they wrote that their research did not support the stereotype of boards wasting whole evenings on trivia. They described these school board minutes as "a record of concerned citizens struggling mightily with a massive influx of state mandates on top of agendas filled with largely substantive, though nonreform related activity" (Nowakowski and First, 1989b, p. 401).

In Table 9.1 are categories of the substantive motions that constituted over 96 percent of the policies passed by sample school boards from July 1986 to July 1987. Each board also averaged three to four procedural motions per meeting to open and adjourn, approve minutes and agenda, move to executive sessions, and the like. Less than 4

Table 9.1

Procedural and Routine Motions Passed by Sample School Districts in 1986–1987

Procedural	Finance/Business Management
Approval of minutes	Bills approval
Recognition of visitors	Payroll
Move to executive session	Claims
Adjournment	Donations and gifts
	Working cash fund
Report approval	Annual budget
Superintendent report	Budget calendar
Board president report	Public hearing budget
PTA report	Transfer of funds
Standing committee reports	Tax levy
curriculum	Public hearing/tax levy
finance	Bond resolution
substance abuse	Building fund data
legislative	Auditor selection
Coop agreements reports	Audit report
special education	Bids
vocational education	photographer
Special information reports	office supplies
Annual report	transportation
	towel services
Personnel	gym floor
General personnel matters	Insurance
hires	liability
retirements	property
releases	auto insurance
leaves	Purchases
Recruitment	equipment
minority recruitment	property
Salary schedule	Investments
Teacher appreciation week	Loss and damage reports
Teacher awards	Contracts
Insurance and compensation programs	school leasing agreement
Staff development	school attorney
salary credit workshops	heating and air conditioning
	natural gas
Students	transportation
Student accident insurance	community use of facilities
Suspensions	food service management
Expulsions	custodial and maintenance
Special programs	program
young authors	Grants
youth soccer	technical assistance

Table 9.1 continued

Procedural	Finance/Business Management
crossing guards	approval to request
Adoption of aptitude test	approval of reports regarding
	Fees
District Policy	textbook rental
Policy readings	pool rental rates
AIDS policy	school rates
Approval of policies	tuition rates
Adoption of board policies	Lunch program
Adoption of board goals	lunch policy
Adoption of school calendar	lunch fees
Adoption of mission statement	lunch supervision program
Adoption of textbook selection policy	Life safety code
	change orders
	safety committee
	recommendations
	Litigation
	vendors

Professional Linkage	Evaluation
Professional memberships	Community surveys
IASB	Special education self-study
NASB	
PTA	
Conference delegates selected	
Conference reports accepted	

Source: Jeri Nowakowski and Patricia First, *A Study of the Impact of Educational Reform on the Schools*. Normal, Ill.: Illinois Association for Supervision and Curriculum Development, Illinois State University, 1989.

percent of the motions concerned reform-related policy issues (Nowa-kowski and First, 1989a, p. 27).

The actions of the boards studied do reflect a response to the state reform act, however. As can be seen in Figure 9.1, particularly in the first postreform school year of 1985–1986, the amount of attention that local boards gave to the substantive-reform areas increased dramatically. The school boards were trying to perform their function of translating state mandates into local implementation. But in the context of political strains and fiscal constraints, the boards had to choose where to be responsive to all the demands on them. The regular routines and obligations of a board do not disappear in the years a state chooses to pass new mandates. The boards varied in their decisions regarding where to be responsive (Nowakowski and First, 1989b).

Figure 9.1

Total Number of Reform-Related Motions, Reports, Discussions in Twelve Sample Districts from 1984–1987

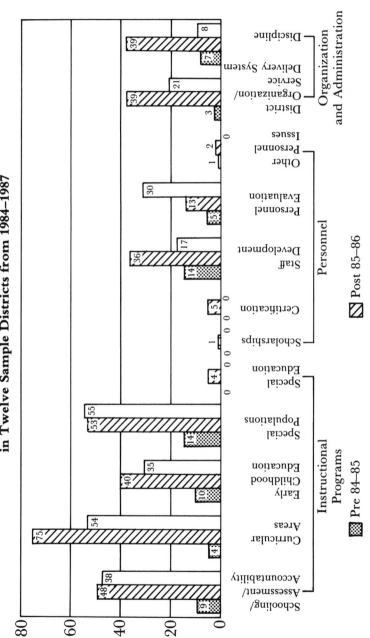

Source: Jeri Nowakowski and Patricia First, "A Study of School Board Minutes: Records of Reform," *Educational Evaluation and Policy Analysis* 11, no. 4 (1989): 389–404.

In a related study in which three kinds of constraints (internal, external, and historical) were identified as preventing school boards from devoting more attention to reform, the strongest constraint was an external one—the need for fiscal support beyond the local district level to implement and sustain reform activities and programs. All Illinois school districts were surveyed regarding what they identified as constraints to a proposed second reform bill to follow the 1985 omnibus reform act. In that study, superintendents overwhelmingly identified financial concerns as the most powerful constraint over six other constraints: labor agreements, state mandates, public concerns, teacher attitudes, time limitations, and district size (First and Nowakowski, 1986).

Also contrary to the belief that local school boards were roadblocks to reform during the 1980s, Allan Odden and David Marsh (1990) report that "local districts, by and large, implemented fully and quickly the major components of state education reform programs" (p. 169). They reported a compilation of studies that looked at local implementation of state education reforms in California, South Carolina, Florida, Georgia, Minnesota, and Pennsylvania. The presence of leadership at the local district level for the implementation of the state reforms in these states was said to be important, but whether or not that leadership came from the school board is not mentioned. The leadership that was mentioned was said to come from "local educators."

Translating state mandates into local implementation is a school board function, as those functions are put forth in traditional lists of the roles and functions of school boards. As Thomas Shannon notes (Chapter 3 in this volume), school board functions include translating federal law and integrating state mandates into local policy action, testing proposed education initiatives against the backdrop of community need and sentiment, evaluating the education program for the community, monitoring superintendent and staff, hearing appeals, dealing cooperatively with citizens, and interacting with other governmental entities.

A growing view is that local districts and state governments are quietly accommodating to their respective governance functions in the 1990s. This notion of accommodation in the post-1980s reform era could parallel the accommodation of states to the federal entitlement initiatives of the 1960s and 1970s. The argument that accommodation has been reached may lay to rest the notion of local boards and districts struggling against state tyranny.

The work of Susan Fuhrman and Richard Elmore (1990) suggests that local school boards have more power vis-à-vis the state than is commonly realized. They write,

New conceptions of state-local relations must account for the ways in which states mobilize public and professional opinion, districts orchestrate state and local priorities around schools and classrooms, and local political entre- preneurs influence state policy. The result is often that the local effects of state policy are greater than one would predict on the basis of state capacity, and localities often gain influence as a result of state policymaking rather than lose it. [P. 82]

It has been suggested that boards adopt a corporate model of board involvement in order to discourage the micromanagement for which school boards are so often criticized. Under such a model, the board's major responsibilities would be the following: the selection, assess- ment, and retention of the superintendent who would truly be given the job of chief executive officer; the enactment of board policy, that is, a comprehensive educational strategy; acquiring and allocating re- sources, but not the details of such allocation; establishing the ex- pectation of program assessment and reporting; and exerting a lead- ership role in influencing state and federal statutory requirements (Brown, Peterkin, and Finkelstein, 1991). This list is reminiscent of the three basic evaluative questions asked of boards by the Organiza- tion for Economic Cooperation and Development (1987), which are noted earlier in this chapter. The holding of fewer meetings, the directing of boards' attention outward as cheerleaders for education, and the refocusing of the board members' attention on the cultivation of good media, community, and state relations are concrete sugges- tions that could accompany the corporate model. A bonus side effect would be the freeing of the superintendent's time from preparing for frequent and long board meetings to enable him or her to provide leadership for the school district.

CHANGING POPULATIONS—CHANGING NEEDS

Much has been written about the changing nature of our country's population as we approach the next century. The population that is served by still largely white, middle-class school boards is becoming increasingly minority and poor. "As serious as the problem of educa- tionally disadvantaged students is today, all of the key indicators generally employed to characterize this population are projected to show major increases during the next twenty-five to thirty years. By 2020, America's school-age population will be poorer, more racially/ethnically diverse, and living increasingly in single-parent households" (Davis and McCaul, 1990). To serve these children, school boards must look beyond their traditional concerns. They must attend to classroom change and to the prevention and remediation of the difficulties such children encounter.

The problems of children at risk are often attributable to factors beyond the school—to problems in the society at large—and so school boards often dismiss the problems of our neediest children. It is true that a large number of children are placed at risk due to forces and factors in their personal lives. But too many students are placed at risk due to factors within the control of the school board: irresponsive and inappropriate curricula, inappropriate or ineffective teaching strategies, unrealistic educational standards, low teacher expectations for student performance, inadequate basic instructional and student support services, an overall school climate that students often perceive as negative, and teacher insensitivity to student diversity.

The plight of homeless children, perhaps the neediest of the needy, plainly illustrates some of these negative factors as these children are turned away from school, which may be their only refuge, or treated unkindly by educators once they are within the schoolhouse door. In evaluating school boards, it is time to ask if they are fulfilling their moral obligation to all the children in their care and meeting, perhaps to start with, a basic criterion such as kindness. Evaluating a school board in moral terms may be more appropriate than the utility, efficacy, and cost-effectiveness models of evaluation borrowed from the business world and applied in the past to school districts and school boards. It may be possible to view some organizations "as moral agents capable of organizing for moral as well as economic purposes" (Schwandt, 1991, p. 63). If any organizations can be evaluated from a moral framework, surely it would be those organizations entrusted with children's lives.

As research offers new knowledge concerning the teaching and learning of all children, school board members should be held accountable if the best of current practices are not being used in their districts. To do less is to do harm to the children in their care. Good intentions alone do not count in this arena. It is often stated that so many school board members are now elected by special-interest groups that it is difficult for school boards to operate from the trustee concept of school board membership in which board members view themselves as representing the entire community and not just the narrow constituency or interest group that helped elect them. But whatever other functions local school boards assume, the needs of our diverse children demand a return to the trustee orientation. Even boards in affluent communities have a moral, educational, and economic stake in what happens with poor minority children.

The Institute for Educational Leadership (IEL), in looking at the future roles of school boards, saw the importance of having boards create linkages with general government and other children and family service agencies as well as the business community. Another priority suggested by IEL was the increased involvement of parents and community persons in the schools. (See Chapter 6 in this volume.) Such an approach acknowledges that school boards alone cannot solve all the problems of at-risk children but that boards are in a position to take the lead in creating the linkages to provide all the help these children need. A focus on the total child is an emphasis of the Boston University–Chelsea plan, which provides child care for working parents, early childhood education, good nutrition, community centers, and values through character education. (See Chapter 4 in this volume.)

A Rand report that looked at urban school districts that function better than most noted that what these districts shared was a united community commitment to improvement. Board members had gathered support for a comprehensive school improvement plan from the business community, civic leaders, and labor unions, including teacher unions. Board members spent time focusing outside the schools to mobilize political and business support (Hill, Wise, and Shapiro, 1989).

These suggestions point to a fundamental change in the orientation and involvement of local boards of education. A continued failure to reap fundamental change may waste billions of dollars spent to provide inappropriate and ineffective education. The cost of the social and economic damage done by continuing in the same old ways may be immeasurable.

TAKING A FRESH LOOK AT SCHOOL BOARDS

New roles for school boards have been suggested and criticisms have been discussed. Nevertheless, studies show that the public values school boards and when presented with alternative scenarios for governance, prefers to remain with what it has (Institute for Educational Leadership, 1986). Since the same public confesses to not really knowing what school boards do but sees them as a buffer between the public and the professional educators, we are left with a puzzle and a need to look again at school boards. The idea of a buffer role for the board is rather provocative. Seeing the school board as a buffer through next-generation lenses leaves us asking, What is the behavior of professional educators that leaves the public in need of an intermediary device? In assessing such a need, we are cast back to the territory of moral questions in evaluation, or more precisely, evaluation for social justice. The public is apparently not confident that they will receive justice from some of the professionals it encounters in the schools. But the attitudes and actions of public school personnel are ultimately the responsibility of the board.

A good evaluative philosophy and practice for school boards may best be built on the belief in, and valuing of, social justice. Local school boards are a peculiarly American invention. "We can think of no more fundamentally American point of departure into inquiries of human affairs than one based on social justice" (Sirotnik and Oakes, 1990, p. 38). An operational belief in social justice as simple fairness could guide school board actions to the trustee mode. Justice in evaluation was treated by Ernest House (1991) in the NSSE Yearbook, *Evaluation and Education: At Quarter Century*:

> Justice in evaluation is also historically emergent. I interpret the establishment of evaluation as an open procedure for arriving at judgments about public programs to be a move toward increased democratic control, though evaluation can be turned to antidemocratic ends as well. In taking educational programs as objects of public decision, evaluation should further democratic control as opposed to hidden control. Such a practice of public evaluation entails that evaluation be socially just as well as true, that it attend to the interests of everyone in society and not solely the privileged. [P. 244]

CONCLUSION

Let us think again about our journey of exploration and discovery aboard the Starship Enterprise and do what the crew would do: reach out a hand of interest and friendship to whomever/whatever is discovered on the planet school board. Let us reframe how we consider school boards by using the four frames suggested by Lee Bolman and Terrence Deal (1991): structural, human resource, political, and symbolic.

The *structural frame* emphasizes the importance of formal roles and relationships, and at first glance seems a suitable way to view school boards and their hierarchically ordered school districts. Looking at school boards through a structural framework, we expect school boards to restrict themselves to their role of making policy and super-intendents to do the managing of the school district, and we are dismayed that all is not always so neat and tidy (First, 1992). Eval-uators have also looked structurally at the place of school boards in the intergovernmental system and have bemoaned their ineffective placement at the bottom of the structure.

The *human resource frame*, with its emphasis on tailoring organiza-tions to people so that people can get the job done while feeling good about what they are doing, seems well suited to an organization that has responsibility for children's lives and is inhabited by highly edu-cated, and presumably highly motivated, professionals. Looking at school boards and school districts through this frame would prompt enthusiasm for school-site management and other kinds of coopera-tive reforms. We would look for a responsive, caring school board and would be appalled to see political wrangling. Evaluators have looked at how boards get along with the superintendent, the public, and among themselves; and by looking through this human resource frame, evaluators have found boards resistant to change and improve-ment.

The *political frame*, which views organizations as arenas in which different interest groups compete for power and scarce resources, might be appropriate for the viewing of school boards, since more and more school board members are being assisted into office by special interest groups. This frame might provide a clear view of meetings and decision making, but one's sense of justice may remain offended by accepting this view to describe school boards, which have such grave responsibilities for children's lives and for society's future.

Perhaps the answer lies in looking at school boards through the *symbolic frame*. By abandoning the assumptions of reality that appear in the other frames, it treats organizations as tribes, theater, or carnival. It may be revealing, or at least relaxing, to look at school boards as we would an abstract painting by Wassily Kandinsky, without preconceived notions of form and substance, but with open-ness to whatever is happening that somehow comforts public and parents because of its existence and because it functions well enough to educate many children. Let us look at school boards as community theater directors look at a good play: What is good that is going on here that we can reproduce in our community and make work in our theater with our players for the happiness of our audience?

Perhaps this symbolic frame will enable us to look at boards in the twenty-first century. A summary of these musings, a "bottom-line" recommendation, is to forget evaluative systems, checklists, and public report cards on school boards. In evaluating school boards, let us begin with the positive assumption that school boards and school board members care about children and therefore about educating all of them well. And then let us simply look to see if the treatment of all the children illustrates that ideal, no matter how the tribe, theater company, or circus troupe effects that outcome.

REFERENCES

American Association of School Administrators and National School Boards Association, *Goal Setting and Self-Evaluation of School Boards*. Arlington, Va.: American Association of School Administrators, 1980.

Bolman, Lee F., and Deal, Terrence E. *Reframing Organizations: Artistry, Choice and Leadership*. San Francisco: Jossey-Bass, 1991.

Boyd, William L. "Balancing Control and Autonomy in School Reform: The Politics of Perestroika." In *The Educational Reform Movement of the 1980s: Perspectives and Cases*, edited by Joseph Murphy. Berkeley, Calif.: McCutchan, 1990.

Brown, Oliver S.; Peterkin, Robert S.; and Finkelstein, Leonard B. "Urban 'C.E.O.'s: Untangling the Governance Knot," *Education Week*, 13 March 1991, pp. 38, 40.

Carver, John. *Boards That Make a Difference: A New Design for Leadership in Nonprofit and Public Organizations*. San Francisco: Jossey-Bass, 1990.

Chelimsky, Eleanor. "What Have We Learned about the Politics of Program Evaluation?" *Educational Evaluation and Policy Analysis* 9, no. 3 (1987): 199–213.

Davis, William E., and McCaul, Edward J. *At-risk Children and Youth: A Crisis in Our Schools and Society*. Orono: Institute for the Study of At-risk Students, University of Maine, 1990.

First, Patricia F. *Educational Policy for School Administrators*. Boston: Allyn and Bacon, 1992.

First, Patricia F., and Nowakowski, Jeri. "School District Response to Senate Joint Resolution No. 26." Report to the Illinois State Board of Education. De Kalb: Northern Illinois University, 1986.

Fuhrman, Susan H., and Elmore, Richard F. "Understanding Local Control in the

Wake of State Education Reform," *Educational Evaluation and Policy Analysis* 12, no. 1 (1990): 82–96.

Garvin, James. "A Community Report Card for the School Board." Unpublished report. New Orleans: Urban Educational Laboratory, University of New Orleans, 1991.

Hill, Paul; Wise, Arthur E.; and Shapiro, Leslie. *Educational Progress: Cities Mobilize to Improve Their Schools.* New York: Rand Corporation, 1989.

House, Ernest R. "Evaluation and Social Justice: Where Are We?" In *Evaluation and Education: At Quarter Century*, edited by Milbrey W. McLaughlin and D. C. Phillips. Ninetieth Yearbook of the National Society for the Study of Education, Part 2. Chicago: University of Chicago Press, 1991.

Institute for Educational Leadership. *School Boards: Strengthening Grass Roots Leadership.* Washington, D.C.: Institute for Educational Leadership, 1986.

Lewis, Anne C. "Presidential Politics and the Schools," *Phi Delta Kappan* 69 (1988): 324–236.

Noblit, George W., and Eaker, Deborah J. "Evaluation Designs as Political Strategies." In *The Politics of Reforming School Administration*, edited by Jane Hannaway and Robert Crowson. New York: Falmer Press, 1989.

Nowakowski, Jeri, and First, Patricia F. *A Study of the Impact of Educational Reform on the Schools.* Normal: Illinois Association for Supervision and Curriculum Development, Illinois State University, 1989a.

Nowakowski, Jeri, and First, Patricia F. "A Study of School Board Minutes: Records of Reform," *Educational Evaluation and Policy Analysis* 11, no. 4 (1989b): 389–404.

Odden, Allan, and Marsh, David. "Local Response to the 1980s State Education Reforms: New Patterns of Local and State Interaction." In *The Educational Reform Movement of the 1980s: Perspectives and Cases*, edited by Joseph Murphy. Berkeley, Calif.: McCutchan, 1990.

Organization for Economic Cooperation and Development. *Quality of Schooling: A Clarifying Report.* Restricted Secretariat Paper ED(87) 13. Paris: Organization for Economic Cooperation and Development, 1987.

Reecer, Marcia. "Yes, Boards Are under Fire, but Reports of Your Death Are Greatly Exaggerated," *American School Board Journal* 176, no. 3 (1989): 31–34.

Schwandt, Thomas A. "Evaluation as Moral Critique." In *Organizations in Transition: Opportunities and Challenges for Evaluation*, edited by Colleen L. Larson and Hallie Preskill. San Francisco: Jossey-Bass, 1991.

Sirotnik, Kenneth A., and Oakes, Jeannie. "Evaluation as Critical Inquiry: School Improvement as a Case in Point." In *Evaluation and Social Justice: Issues in Public Education*, edited by Kenneth A. Sirotnik. San Francisco: Jossey-Bass, 1990.